BONHOEFFER

ABRIDGED

BONHOEFFER

ABRIDGED

PASTOR, MARTYR, PROPHET, SPY

ERIC METAXAS

NELSON
BOOKS

An Imprint of Thomas Nelson

Published in Nashville, Tennessee, by Nelson Books, an imprint of Thomas Nelson. Nelson Books and Thomas Nelson are registered trademarks of HaperCollins Christian Publishing, Inc.

Abridged from *Bonhoeffer: Pastor, Martyr, Prophet, Spy.* Copyright © 2010 by Eric Metaxas.

Thomas Nelson titles may be purchased in bulk for educational, business, fund-raising, or sales promotional use. For information, please e-mail SpecialMarkets@ThomasNelson.com.

Unless otherwise noted, Scripture quotations are taken from THE KING JAMES VERSION.

Scripture quotations marked NKJV are from THE NEW KING JAMES VERSION. © 1982 by Thomas Nelson, Inc. Used by permission. All rights reserved.

Scripture quotations marked RSV are from REVISED STANDARD VERSION of the Bible. © 1946, 1952, 1971, 1973 by the Division of Christian Education of the National Council of the Churches of Christ in the U.S.A. Used by permission.

Library of Congress Control Number: 2014943495

ISBN: 978-0-7180-1616-6

Printed in the United States of America
HB 11.27.2023

Zum Andenken an meinen Großvater
Erich Kraegen (1912–1944)
"Denn das ist der Wille des, der mich gesandt hat, daß,
wer den Sohn sieht und glaubt an ihn, habe das ewige Leben;
und ich werde ihn auferwecken am Jüngsten Tage."

CONTENTS

PROLOGUE

27 JULY 1945, LONDON

We are troubled on every side, yet not distressed; we are perplexed,
but not in despair; persecuted, but not forsaken; cast down, but
not destroyed; always bearing about in the body the dying of the
Lord Jesus, that the life also of Jesus might be made manifest in
our body. For we which live are always delivered unto death for
Jesus' sake, that the life also of Jesus might be made manifest in
our mortal flesh. So then death worketh in us, but life in you.

—2 CORINTHIANS 4:8–12

Peace had at last returned to Europe. Her familiar face—
once evilly contorted—driven out.

The war had been over for two months. The tyrant took his own life in a gray bunker beneath his shattered capital, and the Allies declared victory.

Slowly, slowly, life in Britain turned to the task of restoring itself. Then, as if on cue, summer arrived. It was the first summer of peace in six years. But as if to prove that the whole thing hadn't been a dream or a nightmare, there were constant fresh reminders of what had happened. And they were as awful as anything that had gone before. Often they were worse. In the early part of this summer, the ghastly news of the death camps emerged along with the unfathomable atrocities that the Nazis had visited upon their victims in the hellish outposts of their short-lived empire.

Rumors of such things circulated throughout the war, but now the reality was confirmed by photographs, newsreel footage, and eyewitness accounts from the soldiers who liberated the camps in April during the last days of the war. The depth of these horrors had not been known or imagined, and it was almost too much for the war-fatigued British public to absorb. Their hatred of the Germans was confirmed and reconfirmed afresh with every nauseating detail. The public reeled at the very evilness of the evil.

At the beginning of the war, it was possible to separate the Nazis from the Germans and recognize that not all Germans were Nazis. As the clash between the two nations wore on, and as more and more English fathers and sons and brothers died, distinguishing the difference became more difficult. Eventually the difference vanished altogether. Realizing he needed to fuel the British war effort, Prime Minister Winston Churchill fused the Germans and the Nazis into a single hated enemy, the better to defeat it swiftly and end the unrelenting nightmare.

When Germans working to defeat Hitler and the Nazis contacted Churchill and the British government, hoping for assistance to defeat their common enemy from the inside—hoping to tell the world that some Germans trapped inside the Reich felt much as they did—they were rebuffed. No one was interested in their overtures. It was too late. They couldn't participate in such evils and, when it was convenient, try to settle for a separate peace. For the purposes of the war effort, Churchill maintained the fiction that there were no good Germans. It would even be said that the only good

German—if one needed to use the phrase—was a dead German. That lack of nuance was also part of the hellishness of war.

But now the war was over. And even as the full, unspeakable evil of the Third Reich was coming to light, the other side of things had to be seen too. Part of the restoration to peacetime thinking was the ability to again see beyond the blacks and whites of the war, to again discern nuance and shades, shadows and colors.

And so today in Holy Trinity Church—just off the Brompton Road in London—a service was taking place that was incomprehensible to some. To many others it was distasteful and disturbing, especially to those who had lost loved ones during the war. The memorial service being held today on British soil and being broadcast on the BBC was for a German who had died three months earlier. The word of his demise so slowly staggered out of the war's fog and rubble that only recently had any of his friends and family learned of it. Most of them still knew nothing about it. But here in London were gathered those few who did.

In the pews were the man's thirty-nine-year-old twin sister, her half-Jewish husband, and their two girls. They had slipped out of Germany before the war, driving at night across the border into Switzerland. The dead man took part in arranging their illegal flight—although that was among the most negligible of his departures from National Socialist orthodoxy—and he helped establish them in London. The man counted among his friends a number of prominent persons, including George Bell, the bishop of Chichester. Bell arranged the service, for he had known and loved the man being honored. The bishop met him years before the war when the two were engaged in ecumenical efforts, trying to warn Europe against the designs of the Nazis, then trying to rescue Jews, and finally trying to bring news of the German resistance to the attention of the British government. Just hours before his execution in Flossenbürg concentration camp, the man directed his last words to this bishop. That Sunday he spoke them to a British officer, who was imprisoned with him, after he performed his last service and preached his last sermon. This officer was liberated and brought those last words and the news of the man's death across Europe with him.

Across the English Channel, across France, and across Germany, in the Charlottenburg district of Berlin, in a three-story house at 43 Marienburger Allee, an elderly couple sat by their radio. In her time the wife had given birth to eight children, four boys and four girls. The second son had been killed in the First War, and for a whole year his young mother had been unable to function. Twenty-seven years later, a second war would take two more boys from her. The husband was the most prominent psychiatrist in Germany. They had both opposed Hitler from the beginning and were proud of their sons and sons-in-law who had been involved in the conspiracy against him. They all knew the dangers. But when the war at last ended, news of their two sons was slow to arrive in Berlin. A month earlier they had finally heard of the death of their third son, Klaus. But about their youngest son, Dietrich, they had heard nothing. Someone claimed to have seen him alive. Then a neighbor told them that the BBC would the next day broadcast a memorial service in London. It was for Dietrich.

At the appointed hour, the old couple turned on their radio. Soon enough the service was announced for their son. That was how they came to know of his death.

As the couple took in the hard news that the good man who was their son was now dead, so too, many English took in the hard news that the dead man who was a German was good. Thus did the world again begin to reconcile itself to itself.

The man who died was engaged to be married. He was a pastor and a theologian. And he was executed for his role in the plot to assassinate Hitler.

This is his story.

 CHAPTER 1

FAMILY AND CHILDHOOD

1906–1922

The rich world of his ancestors set the standards for Dietrich Bonhoeffer's own life. It gave him a certainty of judgment and manner that cannot be acquired in a single generation. He grew up in a family that believed the essence of learning lay not in a formal education but in the deeply rooted obligation to be guardians of a great historical heritage and intellectual tradition.

—EBERHARD BETHGE

I n the winter of 1896, before the aforementioned older couple had met, they were invited to attend an "open evening" at the house of the physicist Oscar Meyer. "There," wrote Karl Bonhoeffer years later, "I met a young, fair, blue-eyed girl whose bearing was so free and natural, and whose expression was so open and confident, that as soon as she entered the room she took me captive. This moment when I first laid eyes upon my future wife remains in my memory with an almost mystical force."

1

Karl Bonhoeffer and Paula von Hase married on March 5, 1898, three weeks shy of the groom's thirtieth birthday. The bride was twenty-two. Both of them—doctor and teacher—came from fabulously illustrious backgrounds. In fact, the family trees of Karl and Paula Bonhoeffer are everywhere so laden with figures of accomplishment that one might expect future generations to be burdened by it all. But the welter of wonderfulness that was their heritage seems to have been a boon, one that buoyed them up so that each child seems not only to have stood on the shoulders of giants but also to have danced on them.

They brought eight children into the world within a decade. The first two sons came in the space of a year: Karl-Friedrich was born on January 13, 1899, and Walter—two months premature—on December 10. Their third son, Klaus, was born in 1901, followed by two daughters, Ursula in 1902 and Christine in 1903. On February 4, 1906, their fourth and youngest son, Dietrich, was born ten minutes before his twin sister, Sabine, and he teased her about this advantage throughout their lives. The twins were baptized by the kaiser's former chaplain, their grandfather Karl Alfred von Hase, who lived a seven-minute walk away. Susanne, the last child, was born in 1909. Dietrich was the only child to inherit his mother's fair complexion and flaxen-colored hair. The three elder brothers were dark like their father.

All the Bonhoeffer children were born in Breslau, where Karl Bonhoeffer held the chair in psychiatry and neurology at the university, and was director of the hospital for nervous diseases. The Bonhoeffer house—at 7 Birkenwäldchen—was near Karl's clinic. It was a gigantic, rambling three-story affair with gabled roofs, numerous chimneys, a screened porch, and a large balcony overlooking the spacious garden where the children played.

Their mother presided over the well-appointed home. Upstairs was the schoolroom with desks, where Paula taught the children their lessons. It had been somewhat shocking when she chose to take the teacher's examination as a single woman,* but as a married woman, Paula Bonhoeffer used what she had learned to great effect. When they were a bit older, she sent the children to the local public schools, where they invariably excelled.

In 1910, the Bonhoeffers decided to look for a place to spend their holidays. They chose a remote idyll in the woods of the Glatz Mountains near the Bohemian border, a two-hour train ride south of Breslau. The name of this rustic paradise was Wolfesgründ. It was so far off the beaten track that the family never saw another soul, save for a single odd character: a "bigoted forestry official" who wandered through now and again. Bonhoeffer later memorialized him in a fictionalized account as the character *Gelbstiefel* (Yellow Boots).

We get our first glimpses of Dietrich during this time, when he was four and five years old. They come to us from his twin, Sabine:

> My first memories go back to 1910. I see Dietrich in his party frock, stroking with his small hand the blue silk underskirt; later I see him beside our grandfather, who is sitting by the window with our baby sister Susanne on his knee, while the afternoon sun pours in in the golden light. Here the outlines blur, and only one more scene will form in my mind: first games in the garden in 1911, Dietrich with a mass of ash-blond hair around his sunburnt face, hot from romping, driving away the midges and looking for a shady corner, and yet only obeying very unwillingly the nursemaid's call to come in, because the immensely energetic game is not yet finished. Heat and thirst were forgotten in the intensity of his play.[1]

Sisters Käthe and Maria van Horn came to the Bonhoeffers six months after the twins were born, and for two decades they

---

* She received her diploma in April 1896 from the Royal Provincial School College in Breslau.

formed a vital part of the family's life. Fräulein Käthe was usually in charge of the three little ones. Both van Horn sisters were devout Christians schooled at the community of Herrnhut, which means "the Lord's watch tower," and they had a decided spiritual influence on the Bonhoeffer children.

The eight Bonhoeffer children (circa 1910) and their governess at the holiday home in Wölfelsgrund in the Glatz Mountains. Karl and Paula Bonhoeffer stand in the background. Dietrich is just to the right of the governess, who holds Susanne, the youngest.
(Art Resource, NY)

When Dietrich and Sabine were old enough to be schooled, their mother turned the duty over to Fräulein Käthe, though Paula still presided over the children's religious instruction. Dietrich's earliest recorded theological inquiries occurred when he was about four. He asked his mother: "Does the good God love the chimney sweep too?" and "Does God, too, sit down to lunch?"

The place of religion in the Bonhoeffer home was far from pietist but followed some Herrnhut traditions. For one thing, the

Bonhoeffers rarely went to church; for baptisms and funerals, they usually turned to Paula's father or brother. The family was not anti-clerical—indeed, the children loved to "play" at baptizing each other—but their Christianity was mostly of the homegrown variety. Daily life was filled with Bible reading and hymn singing, all of it led by Frau Bonhoeffer. Her reverence for the Scriptures was such that she read Bible stories to her children from the actual Bible text and not from a children's retelling. Still, she sometimes used an illustrated Bible, explaining the pictures as she went.*

Paula Bonhoeffer's faith was most evident in the values that she and her husband taught their children. Exhibiting selflessness, expressing generosity, and helping others were central to the family culture. Still, their good behavior did not always come naturally. Fräulein Käthe remembered:

> Dietrich was often mischievous and got up to various pranks, not always at the appropriate time. I remember that Dietrich specially liked to do this when the children were supposed to get washed and dressed quickly because we had been invited to go out. So one such day he was dancing round the room, singing and being a thorough nuisance. Suddenly the door opened, his mother descended upon him, boxed his ears right and left, and was gone. Then the nonsense was over. Without shedding a tear, he now did what he ought.[2]

Karl Bonhoeffer would not have called himself a Christian, but he respected his wife's tutelage of the children in this and lent his tacit approval to it, even if only by participating as an observer.

---

* Bonhoeffer well knew the dangers of pietism, but he drew on the conservative theological tradition of the Herrnhüter throughout his life, always using the Moravian's daily Bible texts for private devotions. Each day there was a verse from the Old Testament and a verse from the New Testament. They were known to Bonhoeffer as *Losungen* (watch words), although he sometimes just called them "the texts."

With the values that his wife taught the children, he was entirely in agreement. Among those values was a serious respect for the feelings and opinions of others, including his wife's. She was the granddaughter, daughter, and sister of men whose lives were given to theology, and he knew she was serious about her faith and had hired governesses who were serious about it.

"There was no place for false piety or any kind of bogus religiosity in our home," Sabine said. "Mama expected us to show great resolution." Mere churchgoing held little charm for her. The concept of cheap grace that Dietrich would later make so famous might have had its origins in his mother; perhaps not the term, but the idea behind it, that faith without works is not faith at all, but a simple lack of obedience to God.

The Move to Berlin, 1912

In 1912, Dietrich's father accepted an appointment to the chair of psychiatry and neurology in Berlin. This put him at the head of his field in Germany. It's hard to overstate Karl Bonhoeffer's influence. His mere presence in Berlin "turned the city into a bastion against the invasion of Freud's and Jung's psycho-analysis," in the words of Eberhard Bethge, a close friend of Dietrich's. Karl Bonhoeffer never publicly dismissed Freud, Jung, or Adler and their theories, but he held them at arm's length with a measured skepticism borne of his devotion to empirical science. Bethge quoted Karl Bonhoeffer's friend, Robert Gaupp, a Heidelberg psychiatrist:

> In intuitive psychology and scrupulous observation Bonhoeffer had no superior. But he came from the school of Wernicke, which was solely concerned with the brain, and permitted no departure from thinking in terms of cerebral pathology. . . . [He] had no urge to advance into the realm of dark, undemonstrable, bold and imaginative interpretation, where so

much has to be assumed and so little can be proved. . . . [He] remained within the borders of the empirical world that was accessible to him.[3]

The family's move from Breslau to Berlin must have felt like a leap. For many, Berlin was the center of the universe. Its university was one of the best in the world, the city was an intellectual and cultural center, and it was the seat of an empire. Their new house—on the Brückenallee, near the northwest part of the Tiergarten—was less spacious than their Breslau house and situated on smaller grounds. But it had the special distinction of sharing a wall with Bellevue Park, where the royal children played.

In 1913, seven-year-old Dietrich began school outside the home. For the next six years he attended the Friedrich-Werder Gymnasium. Dietrich did well in school, but was not beyond needing discipline, which his parents didn't hesitate to provide. "Dietrich does his work naturally and tidily," his father wrote. "He likes fighting, and does a great deal of it."

"Hurrah! There's a war!"

With the move to Berlin, their Wölfesgrund house was too far away, so the Bonhoeffers sold it and found a country home in Friedrichsbrunn in the Harz Mountains. They spent the summer of 1914 there. But on the first day of August, while the three younger children and their governess were in the village enjoying themselves, the world changed. Flitting here and there through the crowd, until it reached them, was the stunning news that Germany had declared war on Russia. Dietrich and Sabine were eight and a half, and she recalled the scene:

The village was celebrating its local shooting festival. Our governess suddenly dragged us away from the pretty, enticing market stalls and the merry-go-round which was being pulled by a poor white horse, so as to bring us back as quickly as possible to our parents in Berlin. Sadly I looked at the now emptying scene of the festivities, where the stall-holders were hastily pulling down their tents. In the late evening we could hear through the window the songs and shouts of the soldiers in their farewell celebrations. Next day, after the adults had hastily done the packing, we found ourselves sitting in the train to Berlin.[4]

When they arrived back home, one of the girls ran into the house and exclaimed, "Hurrah! There's a war!" She was promptly slapped. The Bonhoeffers were not opposed to war, but neither would they celebrate it.

For the most part, however, the boys were thrilled and remained so for some time, though they were careful in expressing it. Dietrich's brothers wouldn't be eligible to enlist until 1917, and no one dreamed the war could last that long. But they could at least get caught up in the whole thing and talk about it knowledgeably, as the grown-ups did. Dietrich often played at soldiers with his cousin Hans-Christoph, and the next summer at Friedrichsbrunn, he wrote his parents asking them to send newspaper articles about events at the front. Like many boys, he made a map and stuck colored pins into it, marking the Germans' advancement.

The War Comes Home

In time the realities of war came home. A cousin was killed. Then another. Another cousin lost a leg. Their cousin Lothar had an eye shot out and a leg severely crushed. Yet another cousin died. Food grew scarce. Even for the relatively well-to-do Bonhoeffers, hunger became an issue. Dietrich distinguished himself as especially resourceful in procuring food; he got so involved in tracking down food supplies that his father praised him for his skill as a "messenger and food scout." He even saved his own money to buy a hen.

When Dietrich turned eight, he began piano lessons. All the children had music lessons, but none had showed such promise. Dietrich's ability to sight-read was remarkable. At ten he was playing Mozart's sonatas. The opportunities for exposure to great music in Berlin were endless. When he was eleven, he heard Beethoven's Ninth Symphony performed by the Berlin Philharmonic, under the direction of Arthur Nikisch, and he wrote to his grandmother about it. Eventually, he even arranged and composed.

Most of Dietrich's earliest musical experiences came in the context of the family's musical evenings each Saturday night. His sister Susanne remembered:

> We had supper at half-past seven and then we went into the drawing room. Usually, the boys began with a trio: Karl-Friedrich played the piano, Walter the violin, and Klaus the cello. Then "Hörnchen"* accompanied my mother as she sang. Each one who had had teaching that week had to present something that evening. Sabine learned the violin, and the two big sisters sang duets as well as Lieder by Schubert, Brahms, and Beethoven. Dietrich was far better at the piano than Karl-Friedrich.[5]

According to Sabine, Dietrich was especially sensitive and generous as an accompanist, "always anxious to cover over the mistakes of the other players and to spare them any embarrassment." His future sister-in-law Emmi Delbrück was often there too:

> While we were playing, Dietrich at the piano kept us all in order. I do not remember a moment when he did not know

---

* It was the term they sometimes used for their governess, Maria van Horn.

where each of us was. He never just played his own part: from the beginning he heard the whole of it. If the cello took a long time tuning beforehand, or between movements, he sank his head and didn't betray the slightest impatience. He was cour-teous by nature.[6]

In March 1916, while the war raged on, the family moved from the Brückenallee to a house in Berlin's Grunewald district. Like most homes in Grunewald, the Bonhoeffer home at 14 Wangenheimstrasse was huge, with a full acre of gardens and grounds. It was another prestigious neighborhood, where many of Berlin's distinguished pro-fessors lived. The Bonhoeffers became close to many of them, and their children spent so much time together that they would eventu-ally begin marrying each other.

As the war continued, the Bonhoeffers heard of more deaths and injuries among their wide circle. In 1917, their two eldest, Karl-Friedrich and Walter, were called up. Though they might eas-ily have done so, their parents didn't pull any strings to help them avoid serving on the front lines. Germany's greatest need was in the infantry, and there both boys enlisted. Following basic training, the two young Bonhoeffers would be sent to the front.

Walter had been preparing for this moment since the war broke out, strengthening himself by taking long hikes with extra weights in his backpack. Karl-Friedrich actually took along his physics text-book. Things were still looking very well for Germany that year. In fact, the Germans were so confident that on March 24, 1918, the kaiser declared a national holiday.

Walter left in April 1918. As they had always done and would do for their grandchildren's generation twenty-five years hence, the Bonhoeffers gave Walter a festive send-off dinner. The large fam-ily gathered around the large table, gave handmade presents, and recited poems and sang songs composed for the occasion. Dietrich, then twelve, composed an arrangement of "Now, at the last, we say

Godspeed on your journey" and, accompanying himself on the piano, sang it to his brother. They took Walter to the station the next morning, and as the train was pulling away, Paula Bonhoeffer ran alongside it, telling her fresh-faced boy: "It's only space that separates us."

Walter

Walter was injured by an exploding shell on April 23. The doctors hadn't thought the wounds serious and wrote the family as much, assuaging their concerns. But an inflammation developed, and his condition worsened. From his sickbed, Walter dictated a letter to his parents:

My dears,

Today I had the second operation, and I must admit that it went far less pleasantly than the first because the splinters that were removed were deeper. Afterwards I had to have two camphor injections with an interval between them, but I hope that this is the end of the matter. I am using my technique of thinking of other things so as not to think of the pain. There are more interesting things in the world just now than my wounds. Mount Kemmel and its possible consequences, and today's news of the taking of Ypres, give us great cause for hope. I dare not think about my poor regiment, so severely did it suffer in the last few days. How are things going with the other officer cadets? I think of you with longing, my dears, every minute of the long days and nights.

From so far away,
your Walter.[7]

He died three hours later.

Walter's death changed everything. "I can still remember that bright morning in May," Sabine wrote,

and the terrible shadow which suddenly blotted it out for us.
My father was just in the act of leaving the house to drive to
his clinic, and I was on the point of going through the door
on my way to school. But when a messenger brought us two
telegrams I remained standing in the hall. I saw my father hastily open the envelopes, turn terribly white, go into his study
and sink into the chair at his desk where he sat bowed over
it with his head resting on both his arms, his face hidden in
his hands. . . . A few moments later I saw my father through
the half-open door holding onto the banisters as he went up
the broad easy stairway which at other times he mounted so
lightly to go to the bedroom where my mother was. There he
remained for many hours.[8]

Later, the family received other letters that Walter had written
in the few days before his death, indicating how he had hoped they
might visit. "Even today," his father wrote many years later, "I cannot think of this without reproaching myself for not going to him
straightaway in spite of previous reassuring telegrams which explicitly stated it was unnecessary."

In early May a cousin on the general staff escorted Walter's body
home. Sabine recalled the spring funeral, and "the hearse with the
horses decked out in black and all the wreaths, my mother deathly
pale and shrouded in a great black mourning veil . . . my father, my
relatives, and all the many silent people dressed in black on the way
to the chapel." Dietrich's cousin Hans-Christoph von Hase remembered "the young boys and girls weeping, weeping. His mother, I
had never seen her weep so much."

Walter's death was a turning point for Dietrich. The first hymn
at the service was "Jerusalem, du Hochgebaute Stadt."* Dietrich

---

* "Jerusalem, Thou City Fair and High."

sang loudly and clearly, as his mother always wished the family to do. And she did, too, drawing strength from its words, which spoke of the heart's longing for the heavenly city, where God waited for us and would comfort us and would "wipe away every tear."

Dietrich's uncle Hans von Hase preached the sermon. At the end of the service, Walter's comrades bore the coffin down the aisle as trumpeters played the hymn that Paula Bonhoeffer had chosen: "Was Gott tut, das ist wohlgetan."* Sabine remembered the trumpets playing the familiar cantata and later marveled at the lyrics her mother had chosen:

> What God has done, it is well done.
> His will is always just.
> Whatever He will do to me,
> In Him I'll ever place my trust.

Karl-Friedrich remained in the infantry, and the unspeakable but real possibility that they might lose him, too, compounded Paula's agony. Then seventeen-year-old Klaus was called up. It was too much. She collapsed. For several weeks, unable to get out of bed, she stayed with close neighbors, the Schönes.

In September Dietrich joined his von Hase cousins in Waldau, about forty miles east of Breslau. Uncle Hans, Paula's brother, was the superintendent of the Liegnitz church district there and lived in a parsonage. Dietrich's visit formed part of his connection with his mother's side of the family, for whom being a pastor or theologian was as normal as being a scientist was for the Bonhoeffer side. It was around this time that he began to think about studying theology.

---

* "What God does is done well."

Germany Loses the War

If 1918 can be seen as the year that Dietrich Bonhoeffer left childhood, it can be seen as the year that Germany did too. Sabine called the era before the war a time "in which a different order prevailed, an order which seemed to us then firmly established enough to last for ever, an order imbued with Christian meaning, in which we could pass a sheltered and secure childhood."

In November of 1918, all that changed: Germany lost the war.

The turmoil that followed was unprecedented. Just a few months earlier they had been on the verge of victory. What had happened? Many blamed the Communists for sowing seeds of discontent among the troops at a crucial time. This was where the famous *Dolchstoss* (stab-in-the-back) legend came about. It maintained that the real enemy in the war was not the Allied powers, but those pro-Communist, pro-Bolshevist Germans who had destroyed Germany's chances of victory from within, who had "stabbed it in the back."

The threat of a Communist coup was palpable at the end of 1918. The events in Russia the previous year were fresh in every German's mind. To prevent the same horror from overtaking Germany, a democratic government would have to be formed. It was a high price to pay, but there was no alternative: the kaiser had to abdicate. The people clamored for it, and the Allied powers demanded it.

So in November it fell to the beloved field marshal Paul von Hindenburg to do the dirtiest work of all: he would go to Supreme Headquarters and persuade Kaiser Wilhelm that monarchy in Germany had come to an end.

When Hindenburg left the conference room after that meeting, a seventeen-year-old orderly from Grunewald was standing in the hallway. Klaus Bonhoeffer never forgot the moment when the stout field marshal brushed past him. He later described the exiting Hindenburg as being "rigid as a statue both in countenance and bearing."

The Weimar Republic and the Treaty of Versailles

On November 9 the kaiser saw no alternative and abdicated the throne. In a moment, the Germany of the last fifty years vanished. But the mobs milling around Berlin weren't satisfied. Revolution was in the air. The ultra-left Spartacists had taken over the kaiser's palace and were on the verge of declaring a Soviet republic. The Social Democrats had a majority in the Reichstag, but it could all vanish at any moment. Just outside the Reichstag on the Koenigsplatz the angry crowds clamored for change, demanding something, *anything*— and that's precisely what they got. Throwing political caution to the winds and a cheap sop to the crowd below, Philipp Scheidemann* opened the gigantic window, and without any particular authority to do so, declared a German republic! That was that.

Meanwhile, less than a mile down the street, the Communists, having taken over the kaiser's *Stadtschloss* (palace), were not ready to surrender. They still wanted a full-blown Soviet republic, and two hours after Scheidemann declared "the German republic" from the Reichstag window, socialist Karl Liebknecht followed suit, throwing open a window in the *Stadtschloss* and declaring a "free Socialist republic"! It was in this childish way, with two windows flung open in two historic buildings, that the four-month-long civil war, called the German Revolution, began.

The army eventually restored order by defeating the Communists and murdering Liebknecht. But this impetuous declaration of the Weimar Republic was as imperfect a beginning of a democratic regime as one could imagine. It was a compromise to which no one had really agreed. The right-wing monarchists and the military pledged to support the new government—but they never did. Instead, they distanced themselves and blamed the loss of the war on the republic itself and all other leftist elements, especially Communists and Jews.

---

* Philipp Scheidemann (1865–1939) was a German politician.

But as the spring of 1919 wore on, just as everyone thought things were being restored to something they could live with, the most humiliating and crushing blow of all came. That May, the Allies published the full terms of peace that they demanded and signed in the fabled Hall of Mirrors at Versailles. The Germans were astonished. They had thought the worst was over.

The treaty required Germany to give up territory in France, Belgium, and Denmark, as well as all her Asian and African colonies. It also required her to pay exorbitant reparations in gold, ships, lumber, coal, and livestock. But there were three other demands that were particularly unbearable: first, Germany must give up most of Poland, thus cutting off East Prussia from the rest of the nation; second, she must officially accept sole responsibility for the war; and third, she must eviscerate her military. These demands were heinous individually, but taken together they were beyond comprehension.

The outcry from all quarters was great. It was intolerable. It amounted to a death sentence for the nation, and that it would prove to be. But there was no recourse but to accept it and the deep humiliation that came with it. Scheidemann, the man who had thrown open the Reichstag window and fatuously proclaimed the German republic, now pronounced a curse: "May the hand wither that signs this treaty!" It was signed nonetheless.

The Bonhoeffer family, like all German families, followed the action closely. Living a few miles from the center of Berlin, they could not avoid it. One day a battle between the Communists and government troops broke out a half mile from their house, at the Halensee train station. Dietrich, in the tone of a typical thirteen-year-old boy thrilled to be close to "the action," wrote his grandmother:

> It wasn't too dangerous, but we could hear it quite clearly because it happened at night. The whole thing lasted about an hour. Then these fellows were pushed back. When they tried it again around 6 o'clock in the morning, they only got bloody

heads. This morning we heard artillery fire. We don't know yet where it came from. At the moment it is thumping again, but it seems to be only in the distance.[9]

But Dietrich had concerns even closer to home. In December 1918, he wrote his grandmother: "Mama is doing much better now. In the morning she still feels very weak, but in the afternoon she feels quite steady again. Sadly, she still eats hardly anything." A month later: "So far mama is feeling pretty good again. . . . For a while she lived with the Schönes across the street. Since then, she has been doing significantly better."

Dietrich Chooses Theology

At fourteen, Dietrich and Sabine were enrolled in Paster Hermann Priebe's confirmation class at the Grunewald church. When he was confirmed in March 1921, Paula Bonhoeffer gave Dietrich his brother Walter's Bible. For the rest of his life he used it for daily devotions. It wasn't until that year of his life that he was ready to tell anyone he had decided to become a theologian. It took a bold and courageous person to announce such a thing in the Bonhoeffer family. Emmi Bonhoeffer remembered the atmosphere then:

> To keep a distance in manners and spirit, without being cool, to be interested without curiosity—that was about [Dietrich's] line. . . . He could not stand empty talk. He sensed unfailingly whether the other person meant what he said. All the Bonhoeffers reacted with extreme sensitivity against every mannerism and affectation of thought; I think it was in their nature, and sharpened by their education. They were allergic to even the slightest touch of this, it made them intolerant, even unjust. Whereas we Delbrücks shrank from saying anything banal, the Bonhoeffers shrank

from saying anything interesting for fear it might turn out to be not so interesting after all, and the inherent claim might be ironically smiled at. Such an ironical smile from their father may often have hurt the gentle natures, but it did sharpen the strong ones. . . . In the Bonhoeffer family one learnt to think before asking a question or making a remark. It was embarrassing to see their father raise his left eyebrow inquiringly. It was a relief when this was accompanied by a kindly smile, but absolutely devastating when his expression remained serious. But he never really wanted to devastate, and everybody knew it.[10]

Dietrich's decision to become a theologian was firm, but his parents weren't quite convinced this was the best path for him. He was so talented as a musician, they thought he still might want to turn in that direction. The famed pianist Leonid Kreutzer was teaching at the Berliner Hochschule für Musik, and the Bonhoeffers arranged for Dietrich to play for him and hear his opinion.* Kreutzer's verdict was inconclusive. In any case, later that year Dietrich chose to take Hebrew as his elective in school.

In November 1921, at age fifteen, Bonhoeffer went to the first evangelistic meeting of his life. General Bramwell Booth of the Salvation Army had conducted ministry in Germany before the war, and in 1919, greatly moved by reports of the suffering there, especially the hunger among children, he found a way around the official channels and was able to have milk distributed. He also gave five thousand pounds to relief efforts.

Two years later, Booth came to Berlin to lead a series of evangelistic meetings. Thousands showed up, including many soldiers, broken by the war. Sabine recalled that "Dietrich was eager to take

---

* Kreutzer was a German Jew later targeted by the Nazis (Alfred Rosenberg in particular) as a "cultural enemy," forcing him to immigrate to America in 1933.

part in it. He was the youngest person there, but he was very inter-ested. He was impressed by the joy he had seen on Booth's face, and he told us of the people carried away by Booth, and of the conversions."

But the turmoil of the early Weimar Republic was never far away, especially in Berlin. When Bonhoeffer was sixteen, it came especially close. On June 25, 1922, he wrote Sabine, "I went to school and arrived after the third period. I just arrived when one heard a peculiar crack in the courtyard. Rathenau had been assassinated—barely 300 meters away from us! What a pack of right-wing Bolshevik scoun-drels! . . . People are responding with crazed excitement and rage here in Berlin. They are having fist-fights in the Reichstag."

Walther Rathenau, a politically moderate Jew, had been the German foreign minister, and he felt Germany should pay its war debts as stipulated by the Treaty of Versailles while simultaneously trying to renegotiate them. For these views, and for his Jewishness, he was despised by the right wing, who that day dispatched a carful of thugs with machine guns to murder him on his way to his offices in the Wilhelmstrasse.

Eleven years later, with Adolph Hitler's rise to power, these murderers would be declared German national heroes and June 24 made a national day of celebration to commemorate their deed.

✛✛ CHAPTER 2

BONHOEFFER THE STUDENT

1923–1927

From the time I was thirteen years old it was clear to me that I would study theology.

—DIETRICH BONHOEFFER

I
t was family tradition that all Bonhoeffers begin their university studies with a year in Tübingen. Karl-Friedrich had done so in 1919; Klaus and Sabine had followed. Christel (Christine) was already there, and of course their father had begun the tradition. In 1923 it was Dietrich's turn. Their grandmother Julie Bonhoeffer lived in Tübingen at 38 Neckarhalde, on the Neckar River, and Christel and Dietrich stayed with her for most of their time there.

For Germany, 1923 was disastrous. The German mark, which had begun to slide two years earlier, went into free fall. In 1921 it had dropped to 75 marks to the dollar; the next year to 400; and by early 1923 it had plunged to 7,000. In 1922, unable to bear up any longer, the German government asked for a moratorium on payments stipulated by the Versailles Treaty. The French refused. Germany defaulted. The French promptly dispatched troops to occupy the Ruhr region, Germany's center of industry. The resultant economic turmoil would make the bleak conditions of a few months earlier look like the good old days: by August a dollar was worth one million marks; and by September, August seemed like the good old days.

Toward the end of 1923 a life-insurance policy of Karl Bonhoeffer's matured, paying him 100,000 marks. He had made payments for decades, and now, because of inflation, the reward was only enough to purchase a bottle of wine and some strawberries. When the money finally arrived, it covered only the berries. By the end of 1923, things had become impossible. In October Dietrich wrote that every meal cost one billion marks. He wanted to pay for two or three weeks of meals in advance, but needed the family to send him funds. "I don't have that much money on hand," he explained. "I had to spend 6 billion for bread."

By November 1923 a dollar was worth about four billion German marks.

On November 8, Hitler led his famous Munich *Bierhall Putsch* and was trundled off to jail for high treason. There, in the peace and quiet of Lansberg am Lech, like an exiled emperor, he met with cronies, dictated his manifesto *Mein Kampf*, and planned his next move.

Perchance to Rome

The seventeen-year-old Dietrich often skated on the Neckar River that winter, but in late January 1924, he slipped and fell on the ice, striking his head so hard that he lay unconscious for some time. When his father, the brain expert, learned the details of the accident and of how long his son was unconscious, he and his wife immediately traveled to Tübingen. Dietrich had suffered a concussion, nothing more, and what began as an unpleasant journey turned into a pleasant visit. For Dietrich it was extremely pleasant: it was during this time of convalescence, in which he celebrated his eighteenth birthday, that the utterly capital idea of a semester in Rome presented itself. Dietrich seemed almost to have lost his mind for joy at the prospect.

The day after their birthday, he wrote Sabine. Their silly competitive teasing knew no bounds:

> I received all sorts of fabulous and magnificent things for my birthday. Surely you know about the books. I received something else that you won't even be able to guess at, a splendid guitar. I'm sure you'll be jealous because it has a wonderful tone. Papa had given me 50 marks for anything else I wanted, so I bought a guitar and am very happy about it. And just so you won't get over your astonishment, I'll tell you about the next completely unbelievable occurrence. Just think, it is possible that next semester—I will be studying in Rome!! Of course, nothing is at all certain yet, but it would be absolutely the most fabulous thing that could happen to me. I can't even begin to imagine how great that would be! . . . . [Y]ou can certainly shower me with advice; but don't be too envious while you are doing it. I'm already making inquiries everywhere around here. Everyone is telling me that it is very in-expensive. Papa still thinks that I really should postpone it. Nevertheless after thinking about it, I want to do it so much that I can't imagine ever wanting to do it more than I do now. . . . Talk about it a lot at home; it can only help things. Keep your ears open as well. . . . Best wishes, and don't be too envious.
>
> Yours, Dietrich[1]

In a series of letters quickly following, Dietrich tried to wheedle his parents' approval for the trip—presenting reasons for its sensibleness and trying to hide his giddy excitement. To his tremendous satisfaction, and probably because his brother Klaus would accompany him, they lent their approval. So on the evening of April 3, half-wild with expectation, Dietrich and Klaus boarded the night train for Rome. What Dietrich would experience in the glorious and fabled city would be more important to his future than even he expected.

Because of the distaste for France and England engendered by the war and Versailles, traveling to Italy became especially popular among Germans. But for Dietrich Bonhoeffer, it was the cultural and ancestral pilgrimage of a lifetime.

What Is the Church?

The eighteen-year-old pilgrim kept a detailed journal. On the train, just beyond the Brenner Pass, he wrote, "It feels strange when one first crosses the Italian border. Fantasy begins to transform itself into reality. Will it really be nice to have all one's wishes fulfilled? Or might I return home completely disillusioned after all?" Bonhoeffer spun through Rome like a cyclone, absorbing as much of its culture as possible.

At the Vatican he was enraptured with the Sistine Chapel, and in his diary Bonhoeffer recorded that Palm Sunday was "the first day that something of the reality of Catholicism dawned on me, nothing romantic or the like, but rather that I am beginning, I believe, to understand the concept 'church.'" This new idea forming in the eighteen-year-old's mind that day in Rome would end up having profoundly significant ramifications.

The occasion for his epiphany was a Mass at St. Peter's performed by a cardinal, with a boys' choir whose singing took his breath away. A host of other clergy, including seminarians and monks, was at the altar: "The universality of the church was illustrated in a marvelously effective manner. White, black, yellow members of religious orders—everyone was in clerical robes united under the church. It truly seems ideal." During the Mass, he stood next to a woman with a missal and was able to follow along and enjoy it all the more. He gushed over the choir's singing of the *Credo*.

To think of the church as something universal would change everything for him. If the church was something that actually existed, then it existed not just in Germany or Rome but beyond both.

The openness that Bonhoeffer brought to this idea of the church—and to the Roman Catholic Church—was hardly typical of German Lutherans. But Dietrich had been reared to guard against parochialism and to assiduously avoid relying on feelings or anything unsupported by sound reasoning. For Dietrich the theologian to hold a prejudice in favor of Lutheranism or Protestantism, or even Christianity, would be wrong.

That Palm Sunday Bonhoeffer attended Evensong too. At six o'clock he was at the Trinità dei Monti and found it "almost indescribable." He wrote that the "forty young girls who wanted to become nuns entered in a solemn procession wearing nun's habits with blue or green sashes. . . . With unbelievable simplicity, grace, and great seriousness they sang Evensong while a priest officiated at the altar. . . . The ritual was truly no longer merely ritual. Instead, it was worship in the true sense. The whole thing gave one an unparalleled impression of profound, guileless piety."

During Holy Week, he wondered about the Reformation and whether it went wrong when it officially became a church rather than simply remaining a "sect." In a few years this would become crucially important to him. At this stage, he seemed to be in favor of the idea of a movement that did not become an organized church. In his diary, he wrote,

> If Protestantism had never become an established church the situation would be completely different . . . [it] would represent an unusual phenomenon of religious life and serious thoughtful piety. It would therefore be the ideal form of religion. . . . [The church] must completely separate herself from

the state. . . . It wouldn't be long before the people return because they must have something. They would have rediscovered their need for piety. Could this be a solution? Or not?[2]

Bonhoeffer typically took complete advantage of being in a new place, and while in Rome that Holy Week, he attended morning and afternoon Masses from Wednesday through Saturday at St. Peter's or at the Basilica of St. John Lateran. At every service he used the missal, studying it carefully. He wrote his parents, "The generally dreadful recitation of these texts by the priest and the choir at home leads one to believe that the quality of the texts themselves is equally poor. This is completely wrong. For the most part the texts are wonderfully poetic and lucid."

Somehow, before the semester was over, Bonhoeffer got an audience with the pope: "*Saturday*, audience with the Pope. Great expectations dashed. It was fairly impersonal and coolly [celebratory]. The pope made a fairly indifferent impression on me. He lacked everything indicative of a pope. All grandeur and anything extraordinary was missing. Sad that it had that effect!"

The Ivory Tower and Karl Barth

Bonhoeffer returned from Rome in mid-June and enrolled in the summer semester at Berlin University. Sabine was studying in Breslau and was engaged to a young lawyer named Gerhard Leibholz, who was Jewish. Through Sabine and her future family, the Bonhoeffers would experience the difficulties of the years ahead in an especially personal way.

Bonhoeffer's principal reason for choosing Berlin University was its theological faculty, which was world-renowned and had included the famous Friedrich Schleiermacher, whose presence still hovered palpably. In 1924, the theological faculty was headed by Adolf von Harnack, a seventy-three-year-old living legend. He was a disciple of

Schleiermacher, which is to say staunchly theologically liberal, and one of the leaders of the historical-critical method of the nineteenth and early twentieth centuries. His approach to the Bible was limited to textual and historical-critical analysis, and had led him to conclude that the miracles it described never happened, and that the gospel of John was not canonical. Harnack also lived in the Grunewald neighborhood, and the young Bonhoeffer would often walk with him to the Halensee train station and ride with him into Berlin.

Besides Harnack, three other Berlin professors had a decided influence on Bonhoeffer. They were Karl Holl, who was perhaps the greatest Luther scholar of that generation; Reinhold Seeberg, who specialized in systematic theology, and under whom Bonhoeffer would write his doctoral thesis; and Adolf Deissman, who was Bonhoeffer's introduction to the ecumenical movement, which would play such an important role in his life. But there was another theologian who had a greater influence on Bonhoeffer than any of these, and whom he would revere and respect as much as anyone in his lifetime, who would even become a mentor and a friend. This was Karl Barth of Göttingen.

Barth was Swiss by birth and was almost certainly the most important theologian of the century; many would say of the last five centuries. Bonhoeffer's cousin Hans-Christoph was studying physics at Göttingen in 1924, but after hearing Barth, he promptly switched to theology. Like most theological students in the late nineteenth century, Barth had absorbed the regnant liberal theology of his time, but he grew to reject it, quickly becoming its most formidable opponent. His groundbreaking 1922 commentary, *The Epistle to the Romans*, fell like a smart bomb into the ivory tower of scholars like Adolf von Harnack, who could hardly believe their historical-critical fortress pregnable, and who were scandalized by Barth's approach to the Bible, which came to be called "neo-orthodoxy," and which asserted the idea, particularly controversial in German theological circles, that God actually exists, and that all theology and biblical scholarship must be undergirded by this basic assumption.

Bonhoeffer agreed with Barth, seeing the texts as "not just historical sources, but [as] agents of revelation," not merely "specimens of writing, but sacred canon."

For his doctoral dissertation Bonhoeffer was drawn to dogmatics, the study of the beliefs of the church. By September he had decided to write his dissertation on a subject dogmatic *and* historical: he would write about the subject he had begun puzzling over in Rome, namely, *What is the church?* It was eventually titled *Sanctorum Communio: A Dogmatic Inquiry into the Sociology of the Church.* In it, Bonhoeffer would identify the church as neither a historical entity nor an institution, but as "Christ existing as church-community." It was a stunning debut.

Bonhoeffer had a staggering workload during these three years in Berlin, yet as a theological candidate, he had an obligation of parish work as well. He could have gotten permission to do a minimal amount, since his superiors knew how much academic work he was carrying, but characteristically Bonhoeffer did the opposite, ambitiously taking on a Sunday school class at the Grunewald parish church with vigor and vision. Bonhoeffer became deeply involved in this class, and it took up many hours each week. He became so popular that children from other classes left to join his, causing some embarrassment.

Out of this Sunday school class grew the Thursday Circle, a weekly reading and discussion group for young men he personally selected, which met at his home and which he taught.

Bonhoeffer began to wonder whether he ought to pursue the life of a pastor rather than that of an academic. His father and brothers thought that would be a waste of his great intellect, but he often said that if one couldn't communicate the most profound ideas about God and the Bible to children, something was amiss. There was more to life than academia.

First Love

During these three years in Berlin, Bonhoeffer was something of a loner. But at the end of this period and through most of his twenties, there was a woman in Dietrich Bonhoeffer's life. She has been rarely mentioned in biographies, and even in those cases her name has not been given. Her name was Elizabeth Zinn. They were, by all accounts, in love and perhaps even engaged. For nearly eight years they remained close.

The relationship began in 1927. Like Dietrich, Elizabeth was a theological student at Berlin University. She wrote her doctoral dissertation on the theosophist Friedrich Christoph Oetinger, and one of Bonhoeffer's favorite quotations came from him, by way of her: "Embodiment is the end of God's path." When Bonhoeffer's postdoctoral thesis was published in 1930, he inscribed a copy to her; and when her dissertation was published in 1932, she inscribed a copy to him. During his pastorate in London from late 1933 until early 1935, Bonhoeffer sent all his sermons to her, which is how they have been preserved.

In a letter from 1944, Bonhoeffer described his early love affair with Elizabeth Zinn to Maria von Wedemeyer:

> I was once in love with a girl; she became a theologian, and our paths ran parallel for many years; she was almost my age. I was 21 when it began. We didn't realize we loved each other. More than eight years went by. Then we discovered the truth from a third person, who thought he was helping us. We then discussed the matter frankly, but it was too late. We had evaded and misunderstood each other for too long. We could never be entirely in sympathy again, and I told her so. Two years later she married, and the weight on my mind gradually lessened. We never saw or wrote to each other again. I sensed at the time that, if I ever did get married, it could only be to

a much younger girl, but I thought that impossible, both then
and thereafter. Being totally committed to my work for the
Church in the ensuing years, I thought it not only inevitable
but right that I should forgo marriage altogether.[3]

A Year in Barcelona

The same year he met Elizabeth Zinn, Bonhoeffer passed his doctoral examination and publicly defended his dissertation against
three of his fellow students. All went very well, and of the twelve
doctoral graduates in theology from Berlin University that year,
only Bonhoeffer received the distinction of *summa cum laude*. With
his doctorate, he was eligible for ministry training by his regional
church, but he was still deciding whether to enter the ministry or
remain in academia. His family hoped for the latter, but he leaned
toward the former. That November Bonhoeffer was offered a position as vicar of a German congregation in Barcelona, Spain. It was
for one year, and he decided to take it.

There were many farewells before he left Berlin. On January
18 he met with his Thursday Circle for the last time. They discussed a theme to which Bonhoeffer often returned: the difference
between man-made "religion" and what he called "the real essence
of Christianity." On January 22, he presided over his last children's
service at the Grunewald church.

There were other farewell events, and on February 4 everyone
celebrated his twenty-second birthday. His departure was set for
February 8.

On the evening of his departure there was a grand farewell dinner with the whole family. Everyone was there to mark the occasion:
his parents, his grandmother, all his siblings, and by chance, Uncle
Otto. When the family festivities neared an end, two cabs were
called. With some difficulty he said good-bye to his grandmother,
and then at 10:00 p.m. the rest of them piled into the taxis and the

party drove to the train station. At eleven o'clock the whistle blew and the train pulled away. For the first time, Dietrich Bonhoeffer was on his own. For the next year he would be away from family, and for the first time since he could remember, he would not be a student. Dietrich had set off into the wide world.

CHAPTER 3

BETWEEN THE PULPIT AND THE LECTERN

1928–1929

The religion of Christ is not a tidbit after one's bread, on the contrary, it is the bread or it is nothing. People should at least understand and concede this if they call themselves Christian.

—DIETRICH BONHOEFFER

Bonhoeffer was met at the station in Barcelona by Pastor Friedrich Olbricht, a "large, dark-haired, and apparently very cordial man who speaks quickly and in-distinctly," and who "looks quite unlike a pastor, but is not elegant." Olbricht ushered his new assistant to the creaky boardinghouse that would be his home. The only place to wash up was the toilet, which his brother Karl-Friedrich, who visited later, described as "very like a third-class lavatory on a train, except that it doesn't shake." The three women who ran the boardinghouse spoke only Spanish and that day made an impressive effort to pronounce "Dietrich." They failed.

In Barcelona, Bonhoeffer discovered a world strikingly different from Berlin. The German expatriate community was staid and conservative; it seemed untouched by the dramatic events of the last decade in Germany and was nothing like the intellectual, sophisticated, and liberal-minded world of Berlin. The intellectual dullness and the overwhelmingly languorous atmosphere of Barcelona pushed hard against Bonhoeffer's hyperactive mind and personality. He was amazed at how people of all ages seemed to while away the hours sitting at cafés in the middle of the day, chattering about little of any real substance. When he finally found a Spanish professor with whom he might have a more elevated level of conversation, the man turned out to be bitterly "anti-clerical." Bonhoeffer read contemporary Spanish writers and found them similarly disposed.

There was one activity that Bonhoeffer would enjoy in Barcelona, but could never enjoy in Berlin: the *arte taurina* (bullfighting). Though an aesthete and an intellectual, Bonhoeffer was neither effete nor squeamish. His brother Klaus arrived for a visit on Easter Saturday, and on Easter afternoon—Bonhoeffer preached that morning—they were "dragged" by a German teacher to the "great Easter corrida." In a letter to Sabine, who blanched at the thought of such spectacles, he said he conceded being astonished at "how much more cold-bloodedly I viewed the whole thing the second time than the first, and I must say that I can indeed sense from a distance that there is an allure to the whole thing that allows it to become a passion for some."

Bonhoeffer in 1928.

Ever the theologian, he expressed to her something else that had been going on in his mind:

> I have never seen the swing from "Hosanna!" to "Crucify!" more graphically evoked than in the virtually insane way the crowd goes berserk when the toreador makes an adroit turn, and they immediately follow this with an equally insane howling and whistling when some mishap occurs. The momentary character of this mass mood goes so far that they applaud for the bull and against the toreador if, for example, the latter proves to be cowardly and—quite understandably—his courage fails him for a moment.[1]

Bonhoeffer had gone to Barcelona mainly to serve the church. While there he preached nineteen sermons and ran a children's service. Bonhoeffer's sermons challenged the congregations both spiritually and intellectually. In his first sermon he leaped into his favorite subject, the difference between a faith based on our own moral efforts and one based on God's grace. Along the line he mentioned Plato, Hegel, and Kant, and quoted Augustine. It soon happened that whenever Bonhoeffer was scheduled to preach, the congregation grew noticeably. Olbricht promptly discontinued announcing the preaching schedule.

In letters home, Bonhoeffer mentioned that Olbricht was "not exactly a dynamic pulpit presence," nor did he fail to notice other failings. In another letter he wrote that Olbricht "has apparently hitherto done nothing in the way of addressing the younger generation in his parish." Bonhoeffer proposed starting classes for the older children. Every time Olbricht turned around, Bonhoeffer was initiating something that would make more work for him when the young assistant left. Olbricht scotched the idea.

Bonhoeffer's solo flight as pastor was an undeniable success: every summer church attendance traditionally dropped significantly, but that summer the numbers actually increased. In August Bonhoeffer told a friend: "It is quite a remarkable experience for one to see work and life really coming together—a synthesis which we all looked for in our student days, but hardly managed to find. . . . It gives the work value and the worker an objectivity, a recognition of his own limitations, such as can only be gained in real life."

Bonhoeffer's parents visited in September. On September 23 they heard their son preach on a theme central to him throughout his life, supporting the accurately earthly, incarnational aspect of the Christian faith against the Gnostic or dualistic idea that the body is inferior to the soul or spirit. "God wants to see human beings," he said, "not ghosts who shun the world."

In the fall of 1928 Bonhoeffer decided that in addition to his other duties, he would give three lectures, each delivered on a Tuesday evening: one in November, one in December, and one in February, just before he was scheduled to leave. No one expected him to do that, and one wonders what Olbricht thought of the new initiative. The lectures were extraordinarily ambitious in scope, and touched on most of the themes for which Bonhoeffer would become famous in future years. The first lecture was "The Tragedy of the Prophetic and Its Lasting Meaning"; the second, "Jesus Christ and the Essence of Christianity"; and the third, "Basic Questions of a Christian Ethic."

In the lectures, Bonhoeffer tipped one sacred cow after another. Having dealt with the idea of Christ as no mere ethicist, he proceeded to explain the similarity of the Christian religion to other religions. Then he came to his main point: the essence of Christianity is not about religion at all, but about the person of Christ. "Factually speaking," he said, "Christ has given scarcely any ethical prescriptions that were not to be found already with the contemporary Jewish rabbis or in pagan literature." He must have shocked some of his listeners, but his logic was undeniably compelling.

In November, Bonhoeffer was asked to stay in Barcelona, but he wasn't quite sure what he wanted to do with himself. He had enjoyed his year in Spain and was considering leaving academia for the ministry. But at twenty-three, he was two years too young for ordination. By finishing his second postdoctoral thesis—what was called a *Habilitation*—he could qualify as a lecturer at Berlin University and buy himself some time to choose a path. So on February 15, a year after leaving, he returned to Berlin.

A Leap into Academia

Bonhoeffer returned to a Germany increasingly impatient with the Weimar Republic. Many thought it an unpleasant political hash forced on them by their enemies, who knew nothing of German history and culture, and who wanted Germany to be weak anyway. Parliamentary government—where no party had the power to lead— was a drastic change from the days of the kaiser, whose leadership was unquestioned and respected. For many, the rudderless squabbling of the new system was simply un-German. Many longed for a return to some kind of leadership and were increasingly less fussy about what kind of leadership it should be.

Bonhoeffer's second thesis would become the book *Act and Being*. Bonhoeffer submitted *Act and Being* in February 1930. Eberhard Bethge reckoned the following its "classic passage":

> In revelation it is not so much a question of the freedom of God—eternally remaining with the divine self, aseity—on the other side of revelation, as it is of God's coming out of God's own self in revelation. It is a matter of God's *given* Word, the covenant in which God is bound by God's own action. It is a question of the freedom of God, which finds its strongest evidence precisely in that God freely chose to be bound to historical human beings and to be placed at the disposal of human beings. God is free not from human beings but for

them. Christ is the word of God's freedom. God *is* present, that is, not in eternal non-objectivity but—to put it quite provisionally for now—"haveable," graspable in the Word within the church. Here the formal understanding of God's freedom is countered by a substantial one.[2]

Bonhoeffer was invited to attend the final seminar taught by Adolf von Harnack, then eighty-seven. Bonhoeffer had obviously turned in a different theological direction from Harnack, but he knew that he owed much of what he had learned to him. Asked to speak at Harnack's farewell ceremony, he graciously said, "That you were our teacher for many sessions is a thing of the past; but that we may call ourselves your pupils remains still."

Another significant development of this year after Barcelona was Bonhoeffer's friendship with a wisecracking theology student named Franz Hildebrandt. Hildebrandt became Bonhoeffer's best friend, his first close friend outside the family. In a few years he would also become Bonhoeffer's closest ally in the church struggle. Hildebrandt, too, had grown up in the Grunewald district of Berlin. His father was a renowned historian, and his mother was Jewish. By the German standards of the time, this made Franz Hildebrandt Jewish, which brings us to the thorny issue of Jewishness in Germany.

Luther and the Jews

Many Jews in Germany, like Sabine's husband, Gerhard, were not merely culturally assimilated Germans, but were baptized Christians too. And many of them, like Franz Hildebrandt, were devout Christians who chose to enter the Christian ministry as their life's work. But in a few years, as part of their effort to push Jews out of German public life, the Nazis would attempt to push them out of the German church too. That these "non-Aryans" had publicly converted to the Christian faith meant nothing, since the lens through which the Nazis saw the world was purely racial.

To understand the relationship between Germans, Jews, and Christians, one has to go back to Martin Luther, the man in whom Germanness and Christianity were effectively united. His authority as the man who defined what it was to be a German Christian was unquestioned, and it would be used by the Nazis to deceive many. But when it comes to the Jews, Luther's legacy is confusing, not to say deeply disturbing. At the very end of his life, after becoming a parody of his former cranky self, Luther said and wrote some things about the Jews that, taken on their own, make him out to be a vicious anti-Semite.

At the beginning of his career, Luther was sickened at how Christians had treated Jews. In 1519 he asked why Jews would ever want to become converted to Christianity given the "cruelty and enmity we wreak on them—that in our behavior towards them we less resemble Christians than beasts?" Four years later in the essay "That Jesus Christ Was Born a Jew," he wrote, "If I had been a Jew and had seen such dolts and blockheads govern and teach the Christian faith, I would sooner have become a hog than a Christian. They have dealt with the Jews as if they were dogs rather than human beings; they have done little else than deride them and seize their property."

For much of his adult life Luther suffered from constipation, hemorrhoids, a cataract in one eye, and a condition of the inner ear called Ménière's disease, which results in dizziness, fainting spells, and tinnitus. He suffered mood swings and depression. As his health declined, everything seemed to set him off. When a congregation sang anemically, he called them "tone-deaf sluggards" and stormed out. He blasted his theological opponents as "agents of the devil" and "whore-mongers." His language waxed fouler and fouler. He called the pope "the Anti-christ" and "a brothel-keeper above all brothel-keepers and all lewdness, including that which is not to be named." He blasted the Catholic church's regulation of marriage

and accused the church of being "a merchant selling vulvas, geni-
tals, and pudenda." So it is in this larger context that one has to take
his attitude toward the Jews, which, like everything else in his life,
unraveled along with his health.

The troubles started in 1528 when, after a large meal of kosher
food, he suffered a shattering attack of diarrhea. He concluded that
the Jews had tried to poison him. By that time he was making enemies everywhere. In his last decade, his list of ailments ballooned to
include gallstones, kidney stones, arthritis, abscesses on his legs, and
uremic poisoning. Now his nastiness would hit its stride. He wrote
the vile treatise "Von den Jüden und Iren Lügen" ("On the Jews and
Their Lies"), and the man who once described the Jews as "God's
chosen people" now called them "a base and whoring people."

Three years before his death, Luther advocated actions against
the Jews that included, among other things, setting fire to their synagogues and schools, destroying their houses, confiscating their prayer
books, taking their money, and putting them into forced labor. One
may only imagine what Luther's younger self would have thought of
such statements.

A Year in New York

In June, Adolf von Harnack died. The Kaiser Wilhelm Society held
a memorial service for him on June 15, and the list of speakers was
impressive, as befitted the legendary figure. One of them was the
twenty-four-year-old Bonhoeffer. Speaking on behalf of Harnack's
former students, he declared:

> It became clear to us through him that truth is born only of
> freedom. We saw in him the champion of the free expression of
> a truth once recognized, who formed his free judgment afresh
> time and time again, and went on to express it clearly despite
> the fear-ridden restraint of the majority. This made him . . .

the friend of all young people who spoke their opinions freely, as he asked of them. And if he sometimes expressed concern or warned about recent developments of our scholarship, this was motivated exclusively by his fear that the others' opinion might be in danger of confusing irrelevant issues with the pure search for truth. Because we knew that with him we were in good and solicitous hands, we saw him as the bulwark against all trivialization and stagnation, against all the fossilization of intellectual life.[3]

Act and Being was accepted on July 18, qualifying him as a university lecturer. He gave his inaugural lecture on July 31. Soon afterward, he began thinking about going to America for a year of study. His superintendent, Max Diestel, recommended it since it was impossible for Bonhoeffer to be ordained until he turned twenty-five the following year. Karl-Friedrich had been invited to lecture in America in 1929 and could give his brother the lay of the land.

Still, the decision to go to America was not easy. Bonhoeffer didn't think much of what America had to offer theologically. American seminaries seemed to him more like vocational schools than actual seminaries. But in the end, it made sense enough to go. The decision would change his life.

Bonhoeffer planned to sail for America on September 6. He traveled with his parents to Bremerhaven, and at eight thirty in the morning they escorted him onto the ship *Columbus*. They snapped a final picture from the dock as he waved down at them from the ship's railing. At eleven thirty, the ship weighed anchor.

Nine years later, on December 19, 1939, the *Columbus* would be scuttled off the coast of Delaware to avoid capture by a British man-of-war. Her breathtaking interiors would fill with seawater and she would sink three miles down into the darkness.

 CHAPTER 4

TO AMERICA AND BACK

1930–1932

*In New York they preach about virtually everything, only
one thing is not addressed, or is addressed so rarely that I
have as yet been unable to hear it, namely, the gospel of Jesus
Christ, the cross, sin and forgiveness, death and life.*

—DIETRICH BONHOEFFER

On September 14, two days after Bonhoeffer's arrival in America, a Reichstag election was held in Germany, and the results were shocking. The Nazis had entered the race as the smallest of Germany's political parties, with a pitiful twelve members in the Reichstag. By day's end they had exceeded even Hitler's own febrile expectations, amassing 107 seats, and vaulting in a single bound into being the second largest political party in the land.

Bonhoeffer knew nothing about it. Manhattan at the end of the Jazz Age was a dizzying place for any visitor, even one as cosmopolitan as Dietrich Bonhoeffer. If Berlin exemplified the

Old World–weary sophistication of an actress just past her prime, New York City seemed to exhibit the crazy, boundless energy of a bright-eyed adolescent in full growth spurt: the whole island seemed to be bursting at the seams in every direction, and grinning as it did so.

"There is no theology here . . ."

Bonhoeffer arrived at Union Theological Seminary with a bit of a chip on his shoulder and not without reason. Bonhoeffer had a doctorate from Berlin University and could almost as easily have been lecturing at Union as studying there. German theologians were unsurpassed in the world, and he had studied with the best of them. Not many Union students could lay claim to commuting with Adolf von Harnack.

Yet he found the theological situation at Union even worse than he had feared. To his superintendent, Max Diestel, he wrote:

> There is no theology here. . . . They talk a blue streak without the slightest substantive foundation and with no evidence of any criteria. The students—on the average twenty-five to thirty years old—are completely clueless with respect to what dogmatics is really about. They are unfamiliar with even the most basic questions. They become intoxicated with liberal and humanistic phrases, laugh at the fundamentalists, and yet basically are not even up to their level.[1]

Bonhoeffer had no idea what he was walking into, but the bloody battle royale between the liberals and fundamentalists was in full swing in 1930 New York. In one corner, weighing in on the side of theological liberalism and occupying the pulpit of Riverside Church—a pebble's toss from Union and built just for him by John D. Rockefeller—was the most famous liberal preacher in America, Harry Emerson Fosdick. In the other corner, weighing in on the

side of the historic faith and descried as a fundamentalist, stood Dr.
Walter Duncan Buchanan, who occupied the pulpit of Broadway
Presbyterian Church six blocks south of Union—built with no help
from Mr. Rockefeller, thank you.

Bonhoeffer observed that Union was on the side of Fosdick and
Rockefeller. But in an attempt to be more sophisticated than the
fundamentalists, whom they hated, the liberals had jettisoned serious scholarship altogether. For Bonhoeffer, this was scandalous. He
did not agree with Harnack's liberal conclusions, but he appreciated
and respected Harnack's respect for the truth and academic inquiry.
At Union he found people who would have agreed with Harnack's
liberal conclusions, but who were unworthy to tie the thongs of his
sandals. He conceded that American theological students knew more
about "everyday matters" than their German counterparts and were
more concerned with the practical outworkings of their theology, but
said that "a predominant group [at Union] sees it in exclusively social
needs." In Bonhoeffer's view, "the intellectual preparation for the ministry [at Union] is extraordinarily thin."

He believed that students fell into several basic groups, but

without doubt the most vigorous . . . have turned their
back on all genuine theology and study many economic
and political problems. Here, they feel, is the renewal
of the Gospel for our time. . . . At the instigation of this
group, the student body of Union Theological seminary
has, over the winter, continually provided food and lodging
for thirty unemployed—among them three Germans—and
has advised them as well as possible. This has led to considerable personal sacrifice of time and money. It must not,
however, be left unmentioned that the theological education
of this group is virtually nil, and the self-assurance which
lightly makes mock of any specifically theological question
is unwarranted and naïve.[2]

Another group was mostly interested in the philosophy of religion and gathered around a certain Dr. Lyman, whom Bonhoeffer admired, although in "his courses the students find an opportunity of expressing the crassest heresy." Bonhoeffer said that

> the lack of seriousness with which the students here speak of God and the world is, to say the least, extremely surprising. . . . A seminary in which it can come about that a large number of students laugh out loud in a public lecture at the quoting of a passage from Luther's *De servo arbitrio* on sin and forgiveness because it seems to them to be comic has evidently completely forgotten what Christian theology by its very nature stands for.[3]

His conclusion was withering: "I am in fact of the opinion that one can learn extraordinarily little over there . . . but it seems to me that one also gains quiet insights . . . where one sees chiefly the threat which America signifies for us."

As always, Bonhoeffer did much more than focus on academic pursuits. He wasted no time in exploring the city and all it had to offer, and he did most of it with four fellow Union students: Jean Lasserre was French; Erwin Sutz was Swiss; Paul Lehmann was American; and Albert Franklin "Frank" Fisher was African American. Bonhoeffer's experiences with each of them formed an important part of his year at Union. But it was probably his friendship with Fisher, who grew up in Alabama, that would have the greatest influence.

Bonhoeffer's observations on American churches, especially in New York City, had been along the lines of his views on Union. The one, notable exception was in the "negro churches." If his year in New York had value, it was mainly because of his experiences in these "negro churches."

When Fisher came to Union in 1930, his social work assignment was the Abyssinian Baptist Church in Harlem. When Fisher invited Bonhoeffer to a service at Abyssinian, he was thrilled to go along.

There, in the socially downtrodden African American community, Bonhoeffer would finally hear the gospel preached and see its power manifested. The preacher at Abyssinian was a powerful figure named Dr. Adam Clayton Powell Sr. By the mid-1930s, Abyssinian boasted fourteen thousand members and was arguably the largest Protestant church of any kind in the whole United States. When Bonhoeffer saw it all, he was staggered.

Bonhoeffer searched New York record shops to find recordings of the "negro spirituals" that so transfixed him on Sundays in Harlem. The joyous and transformative power of this music solidified his thinking on the importance of music to worship. He would take these recordings back to Germany and play them for his students in Berlin. They were some of his most treasured possessions, and for many of his students, they seemed as exotic as moon rocks.

They visited Fisher's alma mater, the all-black Howard University, where a young man named Thurgood Marshall was then a law student. Bonhoeffer became deeply interested in the racial issue in America, and that March, when news of the Scottsboro case gripped the nation, he followed it closely. To Karl-Friedrich, he wrote:

> I want to have a look at church conditions in the South, which allegedly can still be quite peculiar, and get to know the situation of the Negroes in a bit more detail. I don't quite know whether I have not perhaps spent too much time on this question here, especially since we don't really have an analogous situation in Germany, but I've just found it enormously interesting, and I've never for a moment found it boring. And it really does seem to me that there is a real movement forming, and I do believe that the negroes will still give the whites here considerably more than merely their folk-songs.[4]

His belief that there was no "analogous situation in Germany" would change soon enough. Karl-Friedrich wrote back: "I had the impression when I was over there that it is really *the* problem," and he revealed that the racism he had seen in America caused him to decline an appointment at Harvard; he feared living permanently in America could somehow taint him and his future children as part of "that legacy." Like his younger brother, he didn't see an analogous situation in Germany at that time, and he even ventured that "our Jewish question is a joke by comparison; there won't be many people who claim they are oppressed here."

All Quiet on the Western Front

Bonhoeffer's friendship with the Frenchman Jean Lasserre spoke to him in a similar way. Lasserre got Bonhoeffer thinking along lines that would lead him to become involved in the ecumenical movement: "Do we believe in the Holy Catholic Church, the Communion of Saints, or do we believe in the eternal mission of France? One can't be a Christian and a nationalist at the same time."

Yet it was not a conversation, but a movie that most powerfully brought Lasserre's views home for Bonhoeffer. The now-classic antiwar novel *All Quiet on the Western Front* exploded across Germany and Europe in 1929. The book sold nearly a million copies instantly, and within eighteen months was translated into twenty-five languages, making it the best-selling novel of the young century. Bonhoeffer likely read the book for Reinhold Niebuhr's class at Union in 1930, if not earlier, but it was the movie more than the book that would change Bonhoeffer's life.

With a rawness and power unheard of at the time, the film pulled no punches in portraying the graphic horrors of the war. It won Oscars for Best Picture and Best Director, but for its aggressively antiwar stance it caused a firestorm of outrage across Europe.

In the opening scene, a wild-eyed old teacher exhorts his young charges to defend the fatherland. Behind him on the chalkboard are Greek verses from the *Odyssey* invoking the Muse to sing the praises of the great soldier-hero who sacked Troy. From the old teacher's lips comes Horace's famous line, *"Dulce et decorum est pro patria mori"* ("It is a sweet and fitting thing to die for one's country"). The glories of war were for these young men a part of the great Western tradition in which they were being schooled, and en masse they marched off to the mud and death of the trenches. Most of them died, and nearly all of them cowered in fear or lost their minds before doing so.

The film is antiheroic and disturbing, and to anyone harboring nationalist sympathies, it must have been at times embarrassing and enraging. As a result, the film was soon banned across Germany and remained so until 1945. In the United States, however, it was on screens everywhere, and one Saturday afternoon in New York City Bonhoeffer saw it with Jean Lasserre. It was a searing indictment of the war in which their countries had been bitter enemies, and here they sat, side by side, watching German and French boys butchering one another. For Bonhoeffer, it was unbearable. Lasserre later said he could barely console his friend afterward. By Lasserre's estimate, on that afternoon Bonhoeffer became a pacifist. In February, he turned twenty-five.

The New Bonhoeffer

Bonhoeffer returned to Berlin from America at the end of June. He had been in New York a mere nine months, but in some ways it seemed a lifetime. His parents had hoped to lure him to Friedrichsbrunn, but even that couldn't compete with what awaited Bonhoeffer in Switzerland. Erwin Sutz had arranged to introduce him to Karl Barth.

Bonhoeffer left for Bonn on July 10. Not surprisingly, his first impressions of the great theologian were favorable. He wrote his parents: "I have now met Barth and got to know him quite well at a discussion evening at his house. I like him very much indeed, and am also very impressed by his lectures."

In one of Barth's seminars—perhaps at that first discussion

evening—a student quoted Luther's famous maxim that "sometimes
the curses of the godless sound better than the hallelujahs of the
pious." Barth, pleased with what he heard, asked who had said it. It
was Bonhoeffer. This was likely the first time they met. They soon
became friends. In the next two years Bonhoeffer visited Barth often.

Bonhoeffer was asked to preach at the Kaiser Wilhelm Memorial
Church in Berlin on Reformation Sunday in 1932.* This was the day
Germany celebrated Luther and the great cultural heritage of the
Reformation. The people in the pews that day expected about what
an American might expect from a July 4 service in a mainstream
Protestant church: an uplifting, patriotic sermon. They expected
to be movingly inflated with pride at the miracle of their German
Lutheran heritage and to have their egos sensitively stroked for the
part they played in keeping this grand tradition alive by sitting in the
hard pews when they might have been doing so many other things.

The sermon that Bonhoeffer delivered instead must have
seemed like a nasty sucker punch followed by a wheeling round-
house kick to the chops.

The Bible texts provided a clue of what lay ahead. The first was
from Revelation 2:4–5. People familiar with Bonhoeffer's preaching,
upon hearing these verses, might well have slipped out the side exit.
On the other hand, if they had been in the mood to be blasted back-
ward by a bracing philippic, they would not have been disappointed.

Bonhoeffer opened with the bad news: the Protestant church
was in its eleventh hour, he said, and it's "high time we realized
this." The German church, he said, is dying or is already dead. He
condemned the grotesque inappropriateness of having a celebration when they were all, in fact, attending a funeral: "A fanfare of
trumpets is no comfort to a dying man," he said. He then referred
to the day's hero, Martin Luther, as a "dead man" whom they were

---

* He preached there a number of times during those years, filling in for his friend, the
pastor Gerhard Jacobi, who became a close ally in the church struggle.

propping up for their selfish purposes. It was as if he'd thrown a bucket of water on the congregation and had then thrown his shoes at them.

For the first time in his life, Bonhoeffer became a regular churchgoer and took Communion as often as possible. When friends visited Berlin in 1933, they noticed a difference in him immediately. He had always loved the philosophical and academic give-and-take of theological *ideas*—but this was something new. Something had obviously happened to Bonhoeffer in the previous year—and was happening still.

Bonhoeffer the Teacher

During Easter in 1932 Bonhoeffer took some of his rowdy Zionskirche confirmands to the family holiday home at Friedrichsbrunn.
(Art Resource, NY)

Bonhoeffer immediately took up his post at Berlin University, giving seminars and lectures. But the change that had been occurring in him would be visible behind the lectern as well. Wolf-Dieter Zimmermann was one of his students from those days and first encountered Bonhoeffer in the fall of 1932. There were only a hand- ful of students in the lecture hall that first day, and Zimmermann was tempted to leave. But for some reason he was curious, and he stayed. He recalled the moment:

> A young lecturer stepped to the rostrum with a light, quick step, a man with very fair, rather thin hair, a broad face, rimless glasses with a golden bridge. After a few words of welcome he explained the meaning and structure of the lecture, in a firm, slightly throaty way of speaking. Then he opened his manuscript and started on his lecture. He pointed out that nowadays we often ask ourselves whether we still need the Church, whether we still need God. But this question, he said, is wrong. We are the ones who are questioned. The Church exists and God exists, and we are asked whether we are willing to be of service, for God needs us.[5]

Talk like this was rare from most German pulpits. From a univer- sity lectern it was simply unheard of. Ferenc Lehel, another student, said they "followed his words with such close attention that one could hear the flies humming. Sometimes, when we laid our pens down after a lecture, we were literally perspiring." Inge Karding, one of the few women students in Bonhoeffer's circle, remembered her first lecture with him:

> My first impression of him was that he was so young! . . . He had a good face, and he had good posture. . . . He was very natural with us students . . . but there was, for such a young man, a certainty and dignity in him. . . . He always maintained a certain distance. . . . One wouldn't have trusted oneself to make a joke around him.[6]

Bonhoeffer had always struggled with the "problem" of being charming. He mistrusted it and wanted the words and logic of what he said to be the only things to which others responded. Nonetheless, a group of students formed around him during this time. Their conversations overflowed the boundaries of the lecture halls and seminar rooms. Some met once a week in Wolf-Dieter Zimmermann's attic room near the Alexanderplatz. It was very crowded, but they would stay for hours, smoking and talking. Bonhoeffer imposed a certain discipline even on these gatherings, as he had with his Thursday Circle. It was no aimless gabfest, but a controlled, serious exploration of questions. The students learned how to take the time to think things through to the end. Around ten thirty they repaired to a nearby *Bierkeller* for more informal conversation. Bonhoeffer always picked up the tab.

One evening, Zimmermann said that Bonhoeffer brought the records of "negro spirituals" he had bought in New York:

> He told us of his colored friend with whom he had travelled through the States . . . he told of the piety of the negroes. . . .
> At the end of the evening he said: "When I took leave of my black friend, he said to me: 'Make our sufferings known in Germany, tell them what is happening to us, and show them what we are like.' I wanted to fulfill this obligation tonight."[7]

Bonhoeffer's interest was not only in teaching them as a university lecturer. He wished to "disciple" them in the true life of the Christian. This approach was unique among German university theologians of that era.

One student said, "Among the public, there spread the expectation that the salvation of the German people would now come from Hitler. But in the lectures we were told that salvation comes only from Jesus Christ." Inge Karding said that Bonhoeffer once spoke to her about the seriousness of saying, "*Heil!*" ("Hail!") to anyone but God. He didn't shrink from political commentary, and from the beginning he never felt what many others felt: that somehow politics was not related to Christian faith.

In August, four generations of Bonhoeffers gathered at Friedrichsbrunn to celebrate Julie Tafel Bonhoeffer's ninetieth birthday. Because Dietrich continued to remain in their midst as he did, the fullness of his life as a Christian pastor and theologian was not hidden from them. His family could not have helped noticing the change that had taken place since he left for Manhattan. But the change was not an ungainly, embarrassing leap from which he would have to retreat; it was by all accounts a deepening consistent with what had gone before. His opposition to self-indulgent emotionalism and "phraseology" was the same as ever; his opposition to the National Socialists and all they represented was the same as ever. In light of all this, his faith, like the faith of his mother, was rather difficult to argue with, however one might have wished to do so.

CHAPTER 5

NAZI THEOLOGY AND THE FÜHRER PRINCIPLE

1933

It's been our misfortune to have the wrong religion. Why didn't we have the religion of the Japanese, who regard sacrifice for the Fatherland as the highest good? The Mohammedan religion too would have been much more compatible to us than Christianity. Why did it have to be Christianity with its meekness and flabbiness?

—ADOLF HITLER

On January 30, 1933, at noon, Adolf Hitler became the democratically elected chancellor of Germany. The Third Reich had begun.

Two days later, on Wednesday, February 1, a twenty-six-year-old theologian gave a radio address at the Potsdamerstrasse radio station. Bonhoeffer's speech was titled "The Younger Generation's Altered Concept of Leadership." It dealt with the fundamental problems of leadership by a *Führer*, explaining how such a leader inevitably becomes an idol and a "mis-leader." Before he could finish, the speech was cut off.

This story is usually told as though Bonhoeffer had bravely put himself forward to speak out against Hitler, whose henchmen ordered the microphones turned off and the broadcast ended. But the speech had been scheduled for some time and was not a response to Hitler's election. Still, the timing of Bonhoeffer's speech, two days after Hitler's election, was uncanny.

The Nazis may have censored the broadcast, but it's also possible that Bonhoeffer and the station manager had misunderstood each other, and he simply ran out of time. It's unclear whether the Nazis could yet control the airwaves as they certainly would in a few years.

In any case, Bonhoeffer was upset that the speech ended prematurely, mainly because he didn't want his listeners to come away with the notion that he approved of Hitler. Anyone who heard the end of the speech would understand that the Führer Principle was disastrously misguided, but since no one heard the ending, Bonhoeffer had the speech duplicated and sent it to many of his influential friends and relatives, along with a note explaining that the speech's conclusion had been cut off. The speech was also published in the *Kreuzzeitung*, a politically conservative newspaper, and Bonhoeffer was invited to give an extended version of the speech in early March at the College of Political Science in Berlin. Such things were still possible in early 1933.

Bonhoeffer began by explaining why Germany was looking for a Führer. The First War and the subsequent depression and turmoil had brought about a crisis in which the younger generation, especially, had lost all confidence in the traditional authority of the kaiser and the church. The German notion of the Führer arose out of this generation and its search for meaning and guidance out of its troubles. The difference between real leadership and the false leadership of the Führer was this: real leadership derived its authority from God, the source of all goodness, the authority of the Führer was submitted to nothing.

Bonhoeffer stated, "Whereas earlier leadership was expressed in the form of the teacher, the statesman, the father . . . now the Führer has become an independent figure. The Führer is completely divorced from any office, he is essentially and only 'the Führer' . . .

> The fearful danger of the present time is that above the cry for authority, be it of a Leader or of an office, we forget that man stands alone before the ultimate authority and that anyone who lays violent hands on man here is infringing eternal laws and taking upon himself superhuman authority which will eventually crush him. The eternal law that the individual stands alone before God takes fearful vengeance where it is attacked and distorted. Thus the Leader points to the office, but Leader and office together point to the final authority itself, before which Reich or state are penultimate authorities. Leaders or offices which set themselves up as gods mock God and the individual who stands alone before him, and must perish.[1]

Forty-eight hours had passed since Hitler's election, but with Bonhoeffer's speech the battle lines were drawn.

Hitler gave a speech that day too. He was just forty-three and had already toiled in the political wilderness half his life. Ten years had passed since the *Bierball Putsch* that landed him in prison. Now he was the chancellor of Germany. The opening words of his speech that day were: "We are determined, as leaders of the nation, to fulfill as a national government the task which has been given to us, swearing fidelity only to God, our conscience, and our *Volk*." Hitler then declared that his government would make Christianity "the basis of our collective morality." This statement, which was a lie, instantly annulled itself. He ended with another appeal to the God he did

not believe in, but whose Jewish and Christian followers he would
thenceforward persecute and kill: "May God Almighty take our work
into his grace, give true form to our will, bless our insight, and endow
us with the trust of our *Volk!*"

Years afterward, Bonhoeffer's father recorded his thoughts on
Hitler's victory:

> From the start, we regarded the victory of National Socialism
> in 1933 and Hitler's appointment as Reichkanzler as a mis-
> fortune—the entire family agreed on this. In my own case, I
> disliked and mistrusted Hitler because of his demagogic pro-
> pagandistic speeches . . . his habit of driving about the country
> carrying a riding crop, his choice of colleagues—with whose
> qualities, incidentally, we in Berlin were better acquainted than
> people elsewhere—and finally because of what I heard from
> professional colleagues about his psychopathic symptoms.[2]

Four weeks later, Bonhoeffer preached at the Trinity Church in
Berlin. It was the first time he had preached since Hitler had come to
power. Bonhoeffer saw the new situation for what it was and was not
afraid to preach what he saw:

> The church has only *one* altar, the altar of the Almighty . . .
> before which all creatures must kneel. . . . . Whoever seeks
> something other than this must keep away; he cannot join us
> in the house of God. . . . The church has only one pulpit,
> and from that pulpit, faith in God will be preached, and no
> other faith, and no other will than the will of God, however
> well-intentioned.[3]

The theme was the same as in his radio address, but now the
altar before which idol worshipers would worship would not have
said, "To an unknown false god." Now everyone knew who the false

god was that would be worshiped. Now the Führer to whom the Führer Principle referred had a name.

The Reichstag Fire

When Hitler and the Nazis gained power on January 31, they still held only a fraction of the seats in the Reichstag. But Hitler knew his opponents were too divided to unite against him. He would play them off each other and consolidate his power with breathtaking speed and a calculating ruthlessness for which no one was prepared. On February 3, Goebbels wrote in his diary: "Now it will be easy to carry on the fight, for we can call on all the resources of the State. Radio and press are at our disposal. We shall stage a masterpiece of propaganda. And this time, naturally, there is no lack of money."

But how would the Nazis "carry on the fight"? First, they would burn down a building. It was a scheme at once foolproof and foolhardy: They would start a fire at the Reichstag, the seat of German democracy. Then they would blame it on the Communists. If the German people believed the Communists had tried to burn down the parliament building, they would see the need for extraordinary actions on behalf of the government. They would welcome giving up a few liberties to preserve the German nation against the Communist devils. So the fire was set.

In his monumental chronicle of the period, *The Rise and Fall of the Third Reich*, historian and journalist William Shirer stated that the fire took Nazi leaders by surprise: "Out at Goebbels' home, Chancellor Hitler had arrived to dine *en famille*. 'Suddenly,' he recounted later in his diary, 'a telephone call from Dr. Hanfstaengl: "The Reichstag is on fire!"'"

A shirtless Dutchman of some mental deficiency was arrested on the spot and accused of the crime, but how he figured into things will probably never be clear. Marinus van der Lubbe was a twenty-four-year-old pyromaniac with Communist leanings, but it's highly doubtful that he was part of a larger Communist plot, as the Nazis claimed. One thing was clear: he had used his shirt as tinder.

Karl Bonhoeffer, Berlin's top psychiatrist, was called upon to examine Van der Lubbe. And Dietrich's brother-in-law Hans von Dohnanyi was named an official observer at the trial. The affair weighed heavily on the family that year. Karl Bonhoeffer visited Van der Lubbe twice in March and six times that fall. His official report, later published in *Monatsschrift für Psychiatrie und Neurologie*, stated:

> [Van der Lubbe] was violently ambitious, at the same time modest and friendly; a scatterbrain, without any demand for intellectual clarity, but nevertheless capable of unwavering determination, incorrigibly closed to contradictory arguments. He was good-natured and not resentful, but he resisted all authority. This fundamentally rebellious tendency was probably his most questionable characteristic, and the one most likely to set him upon the disastrous road which he took. The early conversion to Communistic ideas certainly contributed to the same effect; but the undisciplined elements in his temperament made it unlikely in any case, that he would follow a quiet and orderly pattern through life. Something which was unusual in one way or another was to be expected from him. But he was not for that reason to be regarded as mentally ill.[4]

This clinical and lucid report contained no mention of guilt or innocence, and for this reason Dr. Bonhoeffer received irate letters, presumably from both sides.

Van der Lubbe was found guilty and beheaded at the Leipzig prison, but there was not enough evidence to convict the leading Communists, who were exiled to the Soviet Union and welcomed there as heroes. The trial shone enough light on what had happened to lend credence to the idea that the Nazis had unscrupulously been involved in the fire. But by the time the trial was over, it was all too late. The Reichstag fire had served Hitler's cynical purposes and provided the cover to ensure that his grip on the country was irreversible and total.

Indeed, it was on the very day after the fire, when the Reichstag was still smoldering, that he pressed the eighty-five-year-old President Hindenburg to sign the Reichstag Fire Edict, a decree officially suspending those sections of the German constitution that guaranteed individual liberties and civil rights. The words of the decree, produced and signed into effect before anyone had had time to think carefully about it, made possible most of the horrors ahead, including the concentration camps:

> Restrictions on personal liberty, on the right of free expression of opinion, including freedom of the press; on the rights of assembly and association; and violations of the privacy of postal, telegraphic and telephonic communications; and warrants for house searches, orders for confiscations as well as restrictions on property, are also permissible beyond the legal limits otherwise prescribed.[5]

Within days, Nazi storm troopers were in the streets, arresting and beating their political opponents, many of whom were imprisoned, tortured, and killed. The ability to speak against them in the press was gagged; assembling publicly against them became illegal. But Hitler was not through. To formally and legally place the whole power of the government in his control required the Reichstag to pass the so-called Enabling Act.

The Reichstag was functioning, albeit in a greatly restricted way; this Enabling Act would formally take away its powers—for the good of the nation, of course—and for four years place them in the eager hands of the chancellor and his cabinet.

And so, on March 23, like a snake swallowing its own tail, the Reichstag passed the law that abolished its own existence.

The Church and the Jewish Question

The speed and scope of what the Nazis had begun executing throughout German society were staggering. No one dreamed how quickly and dramatically things would change.

The Bonhoeffers always had access to privileged information, but as the shadow of the Third Reich fell across Germany, much of the information came from Christel's husband, Hans von Dohnanyi, a lawyer at the German Supreme Court. The Bonhoeffers learned that something especially disturbing called the Aryan Paragraph would take effect April 7. It would result in a series of far-reaching laws that were cynically announced as the "Restoration of the Civil Service." According to the Aryan Paragraph, government employees must be of "Aryan" stock; anyone of Jewish descent would lose his job. If the German church, essentially a state church, went along, all pastors with Jewish blood would be excluded from ministry. That would apply to Bonhoeffer's friend, Franz Hildebrandt.

Many were confused about how to respond. The pressure to get in line with the National Socialist wave sweeping the country was intense. But Bonhoeffer knew someone needed to think it all through carefully, and in March 1933, he did so. The result was his essay "The Church and the Jewish Question." The most grievous aspect of the turmoil was the willingness of mainstream Protestant Christian leaders to consider adopting the Aryan Paragraph.

Bonhoeffer addressed the issue of the church's attitude toward the state, first by paraphrasing Romans 13: "There is no power but of God; the powers that be are ordained of God." In other words, governments are established by God for the preservation of order. Bonhoeffer then famously enumerated "three possible ways in which the church can act towards the state." The first way was for the church to question the state regarding its actions and their legitimacy—to help the state be the state as God has ordained. The second way—and here he took a bold leap—was "to aid the victims of state action." The third way the church can act toward the state, he said, "is not just to bandage the victims under the wheel, but to put a spoke in the wheel itself." This, he said, is permitted only when the church sees its very existence threatened by the state, and when the state ceases to be the state as defined by God.

Bonhoeffer added that this condition would exist if the state forces the "exclusion of baptized Jews from our Christian congregations or in the prohibition of our mission to the Jews." He went on to say that to "confess Christ" meant to do so to Jews as well as to Gentiles. He declared it vital for the church to attempt to bring the Messiah of the Jews to the Jewish people who did not yet know him. If Hitler's laws were adopted, this would be impossible. It was the spring of 1933, and already Bonhoeffer was declaring it the duty of the church to stand up for the Jews.

"Where books are burned . . ."

One week after passage of the Enabling Act, Hitler declared a boycott of Jewish stores across Germany. The stated purpose was stopping the international press, which the Nazis maintained was controlled by the Jews, from printing lies about the Nazi regime. Goebbels spoke at a rally in Berlin that day, fulminating against the "Jewish atrocity propaganda," and everywhere across Germany SA men intimidated shoppers from entering Jewish-owned stores, whose windows had been daubed in black or yellow paint with stars of David and the word *Jude* (Jew). The SA also handed out pamphlets and held placards: *"Deutsche Wehrt Euch! Kauft Nicht Bei Juden!"* ("Germans, protect yourselves! Don't buy from Jews!")

Bonhoeffer's Jewish brother-in-law, Gerhard Leibholz, was a lawyer, and like many German Jews, a baptized Christian. Karl and Paula Bonhoeffer went to Göttingen to be with Sabine and Gerhard that weekend, while other family members checked in via telephone. On the day of the boycott in Berlin, Dietrich's grandmother was shopping. The patrician ninety-year-old was not about to be told where to shop. When SA men tried to restrain her from entering one store, she informed them that she would shop where she liked and did so. Later that day she did the same at the famous Kaufhaus des Westens, the world's largest department store, ignoring the kickline of SA men stationed in front.

Sabine stayed in close contact with her family. Gerhard was a popular professor of law at Göttingen, so it wasn't long before they were directly affected by the mounting anti-Semitism. At one point, the National Socialist student leaders in Göttingen called for a boycott of his classes. Sabine recalled:

> I had often heard my husband's lectures and I went to the university on the actual day of the boycott in order to be there and to hear what the students would have to say. A few students were standing there in SA uniform, straddling the doorway in their jackboots as only these SA men could and not allowing anyone to enter. "Leibholz must not lecture, he is a Jew. The lectures are not taking place." Obediently the students went home. A corresponding notice had been posted on the blackboard.[6]

After a while, Sabine and Gerhard needed only to walk down the street in Göttingen to breathe the poisonous atmosphere. People who recognized them crossed to the other side to avoid them. "In Göttingen," Sabine said, "many tried to collaborate. Lecturers who had not achieved further promotion now saw their opportunity." But a few were sickened at what was taking place and were not afraid to express their horror. The theologian Walter Bauer met them on the street and launched into a tirade against Hitler. When Gerhard lost his position, another professor approached him and, with tears in his eyes, said, "Sir, you are my colleague and I am ashamed to be a German."

Many of Gert's relatives lost their jobs too. One Jewish school friend committed suicide. There was constant news of this sort.

Throughout 1933, the Nazis continued their campaign to legally bar Jews from state-affiliated institutions. On April 22, Jews were prohibited from serving as patent lawyers, and Jewish doctors from working in institutions with state-run insurance. On April 25, strict limits were placed on how many Jewish children could attend public schools. On May 6, the laws were expanded to include all honorary university professors, lecturers, and notaries. In June all Jewish dentists and dental technicians were prohibited from working within state-run insurance institutions. By the fall, the laws included the spouses of non-Aryans. On September 29, Jews were banned from all cultural and entertainment activities, including the worlds of film, theater, literature, and the arts. In October all newspapers were placed under Nazi control, expelling Jews from the world of journalism.

Karl Bonhoeffer would remain at the University of Berlin another five years; only with some effort did he manage to avoid displaying a portrait of Hitler. Anti-Semitism had existed for decades among the students of German universities, but now they expressed it formally. That spring the German Students Association planned to celebrate an "Action against the un-German Spirit" on May 10.* At 11:00 p.m. thousands of students gathered in every university town across Germany. From Heidelberg to Tübingen to Freiburg to Göttingen, where the Leibholzes lived, they marched in torchlight parades and were then whipped into wild-eyed enthusiasm as Nazi officials raved about the glories of what the brave young men and women of Germany were about to do. At midnight the whole thing roared to grand effect in a great *Säuberung* (cleansing) where

---

* It's unclear whether that date was chosen to mark the end of the Franco-Prussian War in 1871, but since that is the day Germany defeated France and marked the beginning of its emergence as a united Germany, it's likely.

huge bonfires were lit and into which the students hurled thousands of books. Thus Germany would be "purged" of the pernicious "un-German" thoughts of authors such as Helen Keller, Jack London, H. G. Wells, Albert Einstein, and Thomas Mann.

A plaque at the Berlin Opernplatz on the site where 30,000 students gathered at midnight to burn the books of "un-German" authors. On the left is a quote from the German poet Heinrich Heine: "Where books are burned, they will, in the end, burn people, too." On the right: "In the middle of this plaza on May 10, 1933 Nazi students burned the works of hundreds of authors, publishers, philosophers, and scientists."

(Eric Metaxas photo)

In 1821, in his play *Almansor*, the German poet Heinrich Heine wrote the chilling words: *"Dort, wo man Bücher verbrennt, verbrennt man am Ende auch Menschen."* Heine was a German Jew who converted to Christianity, and his words were a grim prophecy, meaning, "Where books are burned, they will, in the end, burn people, too." That night across Germany his books were among those thrown into the crackling flames. Sigmund Freud, whose books were also burned that night, made a similar remark: "Only our books? In earlier times they would have burned us with them."

In Berlin the torchlight procession began at the Hegelplatz behind Berlin University, went through the university, and then eastward along Unter den Linden. The "anti-German" books followed in a truck, and at the Opernplatz stood the great pile of wood that would become the bonfire. Then addressing the thirty thousand, the vampiric homunculus Joseph Goebbels ranted into the darkness: "German men and women! The age of arrogant Jewish intellectualism is now at an end! . . . You are doing the right thing at this midnight hour—to consign to the flames the unclean spirit of the past. This is a great, powerful, and symbolic act. . . . Out of these ashes the phoenix of a new age will arise. . . . O Century! O Science! It is a joy to be alive!"

As with so much else in the Third Reich, the scene had an undeniably macabre aspect to it: the midnight bonfire feeding like a succubus on the noble thoughts and words of great men and women. Goebbels, the propagandist, well knew that to stage a torchlight parade, followed by a bonfire at the stroke of midnight, evoked something ancient and tribal and pagan and invoked the gods of the German *Volk*, who represented strength and ruthlessness and blood and soil. It's no mistake that in the cities where the event was canceled by rain, it was rescheduled for June 21, the summer solstice.

The Future of the *Reichskirche*

In 1933, Hitler never hinted that he was capable of taking a stand against the churches. Most pastors were quite convinced that Hitler was on their side, partly because he had a record of pro-Christian statements that reached back to the first days of his political life. In a 1922 speech, he called Jesus "our greatest Aryan hero." Reconciling the idea of the Jewish Jesus as an Aryan hero is no less preposterous than trying to reconcile Hitler's ideal of the ruthless, immoral

Nietzchean *Übermensch* with the humble, self-sacrificing Christ. Since Hitler had no religion other than himself, his opposition to Christianity and the church was less ideological than practical.

That was not the case for many leaders of the Third Reich. Alfred Rosenberg, Martin Bormann, Heinrich Himmler, Reinhard Heydrich, and others were bitterly anti-Christian and were ideologically opposed to Christianity. They wanted to replace it with a religion of their own devising. Under their leadership, said Shirer, "the Nazi regime intended eventually to destroy Christianity in Germany, if it could, and substitute the old paganism of the early tribal Germanic gods and the new paganism of the Nazi extremists."

Himmler was the head of the SS and was aggressively anti-Christian. Very early on, he barred clergy from serving in the SS. In 1935 he ordered every SS member to resign leadership in religious organizations. The next year he forbade SS musicians to participate in religious services, even out of uniform. Soon afterward he forbade SS members to attend church services. For Himmler, the SS was itself a religion, and its members postulants in its priesthood.

Rosenberg was one of the Nazi leaders most active in creating this "new religion." Rosenberg was an "outspoken pagan" who, during the war, developed a thirty-point program for the *"Nationale Reichskirche."* That it was entrusted to an outspoken pagan shows how much respect Hitler had for the Christian church and its doctrines. Rosenberg's plan is some of the clearest proof that exists of the Nazis' ultimate plans for the churches. A few points of his program illustrate what Hitler was open to approving and, under cover of war, would move toward:

13. The National Church demands immediate cessation of the publishing and dissemination of the Bible in Germany.

14. The National Church declares that to it, and therefore to the German nation, it has been decided that the

Fuehrer's *Mein Kampf* is the greatest of all documents.
It . . . not only contains the greatest but it embodies the
purest and truest ethics for the present and future life of
our nation.

18. The National Church will clear away from its altars all
    crucifixes, Bibles and pictures of saints.

19. On the altars there must be nothing but *Mein Kampf*
    (to the German nation and therefore to God the most
    sacred book) and to the left of the altar a sword.

30. On the day of its foundation, the Christian Cross
    must be removed from all churches, cathedrals and
    chapels . . . and it must be superseded by the only
    unconquerable symbol, the swastika.

The Rise of the "German Christians"

There was at this time a group of pastors who stood solidly behind
Hitler's rise to power and blithely tossed two millennia of Christian
orthodoxy overboard. They wanted a strong, unified Reichskirche and
a "Christianity" that was strong and masculine, and that would stand
up to and defeat the godless and degenerate forces of Bolshevism.
They boldly called themselves *die Deutsche Christen:* the German
Christians. The German Christians wanted a unified German church
in accord with Nazi principles.

In these first tumultuous days of April 1933, the German
Christians held a conference in Berlin. It was a disturbing spectacle
for anyone wary of Hitler's zeal to reorder German society. The
lines between church and state were being blurred aggressively.

Hermann Göring gave a speech to great acclaim, casting the
reordering of society as mainly an "administrative" change. He
refreshed the crowd on the basics of the Führer Principle and
exhorted them to expect their Führer to *führ* (lead) in every aspect
of German life, including the church. As part of the administrative

overhaul, Göring explained that Hitler was proposing the office of a
Reichsbischof, a man who could bring all the disparate elements in the
German church together. Hitler's choice for this position was one
Ludwig Müller, a coarse former naval chaplain.

In her book *Twisted Cross: The German Christian Movement in the Third
Reich*, Doris Bergen wrote that "the 'German Christians' preached
Christianity as the polar opposite of Judaism, Jesus as the arch anti-
semite, and the cross as the symbol of war against Jews." Fusing
the German *Volk* (people) with the German *Kirche* (church) meant
stretching and twisting the definitions of both. Step one was to
define *Germanness* as inherently in opposition to *Jewishness*. To make
Christianity one with Germanness meant purging it of everything
Jewish. It was an absurd project.

For starters, they decided the Old Testament must go. It was
obviously too Jewish. At one German Christians' gathering in Bavaria,
the speaker ridiculed the Old Testament as a saga of racial defile-
ment. His remark that "Moses in his old age had married a Negro
woman" drew boisterous laughter and enthusiastic applause. One of
the leaders, Georg Schneider, called the whole Old Testament "a
cunning Jewish conspiracy." He went on: "Into the oven, with the
part of the Bible that glorifies the Jews, so eternal flames will con-
sume that which threatens our people."

By 1937, a group of German Christians would state that the
written word of Scripture was the problem. "Whereas the Jews were
the first to write out their faith," they said, "Jesus never did so." True
"German" Christianity must therefore move beyond written words.

Their efforts became more and more ridiculous. German
Christians sometimes spoke of baptism as a baptism not into the
body of Christ, but into "the community of the *Volk*" and into the
Weltanschauung of the Führer. Communion presented other difficulties.
One pastor spoke of the bread symbolizing "the body of the earth
that, firm and strong, remains true to the German soil," and the wine
was "the blood of the earth." The paganism of it all escaped them.

Ludwig Müller, the man whom Hitler would put forward as his choice to lead a "united German church" in the new position of Reichsbischof, declared that the "love" of the German Christians had a "hard, warrior-like face. It hates everything soft and weak because it knows that all life can only then remain healthy and fit for life when everything antagonistic to life, the rotten and the in-decent, is cleared out of the way and destroyed."

One German Christian leader, Reinhold Krause, said that Martin Luther had left Germans with "a priceless legacy: the completion of the German Reformation in the Third Reich!" If Luther could break away from the Catholic Church, it followed that nothing was written in stone. This was the weed in the garden of Protestantism. After four hundred years of taking for granted that all Germans were Lutheran Christians, no one really knew what Christianity was anymore.

CHAPTER 6

THE CHURCH STRUGGLE

1933–1935

If you board the wrong train it is no use running along the corridor in the opposite direction.

—DIETRICH BONHOEFFER

At first the German Christians were careful about hiding their most radical beliefs from the German people. To the casual observer, their conference in April 1933 was a model of theological sobriety. But the German Christians were vocal that the German church must be united as a Reichskirche. Anything else smacked of the fractured Reichstag and the Weimar Republic. As a result of the April conference, many Germans were open to a single Reichskirche.

Pastor Martin Niemöller had been a U-boat captain during the First War, and had been awarded the Iron Cross for his bravery. He had initially welcomed the Nazis, hailing them as the heroes who would restore Germany's dignity, chase the Communists from the country, and restore moral order. Niemöller met with Hitler

73

privately in 1932, and Hitler had given him his personal assurance
that he would keep his hands off the churches and would never
institute pogroms against the Jews.

But when Niemöller finally turned against Hitler, he did so fear-
lessly, and the sermons he gave at his overfilled church in Dahlem,
a working-class section of Berlin, were listened to with the greatest interest, not least by members of the Gestapo. Niemöller knew
this and mocked them openly from the pulpit. It was thought that
if ever anyone outside the military could lead a movement against
Hitler, Niemöller was the man. Around May of 1933, Niemöller met
Bonhoeffer and began to play a central role in the church struggle.

Amazingly, on June 18, in the midst of the turmoil, Franz
Hildebrandt was ordained. Because he was a Jew, the question of his
future in the church could not have been more pressing. Bonhoeffer
was there for the ceremony, which took place in the historic
Nikolaikirche in Berlin.

The German Christians held a meeting at Berlin University
on June 19. Bonhoeffer and many of his students attended, but
Bonhoeffer didn't make any statements. He let his students argue
with them. He and his students had planned to walk out en masse
if the German Christians again proposed electing Hitler's Ludwig
Müller as Reichsbischof, which they did. At that point Bonhoeffer
and his contingent stood and made for the exits. To Bonhoeffer's
surprise, 90 percent of the people in the meeting walked out too.

On June 28, Müller ordered SA troops to occupy the church
offices in Berlin. On July 2, an SA commando arrested a pastor.
Those in the opposition held prayers of atonement and called for
prayers of intercession, but Bonhoeffer and Hildebrandt saw another
possibility: they suggested that the churches effectively go on strike
against the state to assert their independence. If the state did not
pull back and let the church be the church, the church would cease
behaving like the state church and would, among other things, stop
performing funerals. It was a brilliant solution.

But as would always be the case, their suggestion was too strong and too dramatic for most of the conciliatory leaders. The theologically compromised Protestants now balked. They couldn't muster the will to do anything as stark and scandalous as staging a strike, and the opportunity was lost.

The Church Elections

Meanwhile, Hitler was moving ahead with his own plans for the church. He knew quite well how to deal with these Protestant pastors. "You can do anything you want with them," he once remarked. "They will submit . . . they are insignificant little people, submissive as dogs, and they sweat with embarrassment when you talk to them." With the cynicism he brought to every call for an "election," Hitler suddenly announced new church elections to be held July 23. This created an illusion of choice, but with the powers at the Nazis' disposal, there was little question who would win.

Despite the stacked odds, Bonhoeffer threw himself into the task. The Young Reformation movement chose candidates, and Bonhoeffer and his students wrote campaign leaflets and duplicated them.

In the meantime, as the German Christians and the Young Reformation movement campaigned for the election, Hitler showed that he knew how to deal with the Catholics too. Indeed, he had been dealing with them privately. On July 20 he victoriously announced that a Concordat had been forged between the German Reich and the Vatican. It was a major public relations coup, since it gave the impression that he was reasonable on these matters and posed no threat to the churches. The first article of the Concordat stated:

> The German Reich guarantees freedom of profession and public practice of the Catholic religion. It acknowledges the right of the Catholic Church, within the framework of the

laws valid for all, to manage and regulate its own affairs inde-
pendently, and, within the framework of its own competence,
to issue binding laws and ordinances for its members.[1]

These would be exposed as weasel words within a few years,
but for now they did their job, holding off criticism and presenting
a pacific face to the skeptical world.

Three days later the church elections were held. It was a
predictable landslide, with the German Christians receiving about
70 percent of the votes. Ludwig Müller was elected Reichsbischof.

The Bethel Confession

Bonhoeffer received an invitation from Theodor Heckel to become
the pastor of a German-speaking congregation in London. Heckel,
who knew Bonhoeffer through ecumenical contacts, was head of
the church's Foreign Office, which oversaw all German-speaking
parishes abroad—what they called "the diaspora."

Bonhoeffer left for London after the election and on July 30
preached to the two congregations considering him. Heckel glow-
ingly recommended him to the departing pastors as someone "whom
I personally feel to be quite outstanding." He also mentioned that
Bonhoeffer spoke "a number of languages" and "has in addition a
special Pauline advantage in that he is unmarried." Heckel's warm
feelings toward Bonhoeffer would change soon enough.

Bonhoeffer and the others in the Young Reformation now proposed to create a clear statement of faith—a "Confession of Faith"—
to force the German Christians to define themselves. Niemöller
played a large part in persuading them to take this tack:

Is there theologically a fundamental difference between the
teachings of the Reformation and those proclaimed by the
"German Christians"? We fear: Yes!—They say: No! This lack

of clarity must be cleared up by a confession for our time. If this doesn't come from the other side—and there's no sign of it coming soon—then it must come from us; and it has to come in such a way that the others must say Yes or No to it.[2]

After the London sojourn, Bonhoeffer went to Bethel community in Biesenthal to work on the confession. As much as he had heard about this fabled place, he was quite unprepared for what he saw. Bethel (Hebrew for "house of God") had begun in 1867 as a Christian community for people with epilepsy, but by 1900 included several facilities that cared for sixteen hundred disabled persons. Bonhoeffer had never seen anything like it. It was the gospel made visible, a fairy-tale landscape of grace, where the weak and helpless were cared for in a palpably Christian atmosphere. Yet even in 1933, the anti-gospel of Hitler was moving toward the legal murder of these people who, like the Jews, were categorized as unfit, as a drain on Germany. The terms increasingly used to describe these people with disabilities were *useless eaters* and *life unworthy of life.*

The chief goal in writing the Bethel Confession was to spell out the basics of the true and historic Christian faith, which contrasted with Ludwig Müller's facile and inchoate "theology." Bonhoeffer and Hermann Sasse had the task of making the distinctions between the two sides crisp and clear.

After three weeks of work, Bonhoeffer was satisfied, but then the document was sent to twenty eminent theologians for their comments. By the time they were through, every bright line was blurred; every sharp edge of difference filed down; and every point blunted. Bonhoeffer was so horrified that he refused to work on the final draft. When it was completed, he refused to sign it. It even contained a fawning line about "joyful collaboration" between church and state. The Bethel Confession had become a magnificent waste of words.

The Aryan Paragraph
and the Pastors' Emergency League

Bonhoeffer decided to accept the offer to pastor the German-speaking congregations in London. Before leaving, he circulated a pamphlet he had written, called "The Aryan Paragraph in the Church," laying out his position, especially in light of the developments since April, when he had written "The Church and the Jewish Question." In the pamphlet he rebutted the idea behind the "orders of creation" theology of the German Christians in which "ethnicity" was sacred and inviolable, and he rebutted the idea that the "opportunity for evangelism" that came of excluding Jews was worth anything. He also suggested that German clergy could no longer reasonably serve a church in which they were accorded special privileges over clergy of Jewish descent. When the pamphlet was brought to the attention of Theodor Heckel, it was decided that unless he recanted his position, they would not send Bonhoeffer to London to represent the German church.

A national synod was held in Berlin on September 5. It was overwhelmingly dominated by the German Christians, and 80 percent of the delegates wore the brown shirts of the Nazi uniform. It became known as the Brown Synod, and was less like a synod than a Nazi rally. The Aryan Paragraph was officially adopted.

For Bonhoeffer and Hildebrandt, the time for schism had arrived. A church synod had officially voted to exclude a group of persons from Christian ministry simply because of their ethnic background. Bonhoeffer and Hildebrandt called for the pastors to stand up and be counted by resigning from office. But they were voices crying in the wilderness. No one else was willing to go that far just yet.

Nonetheless, it was in reaction to the Brown Synod that the soon-to-be-famous *Pfarrernotbund* (Pastors' Emergency League) came into being. Bonhoeffer and Hildebrandt could not persuade the others that now was the time for resignations and schism, but on

September 7 they drew up an official protest to the Brown Synod titled "To the National Synod." The statement contained four main points. First, it declared that its signers would rededicate themselves to the Scriptures and to the previous doctrinal confessions of the church. Second, they would work to protect the church's fidelity to Scripture and to the confessions. Third, they would lend financial aid to those being persecuted by the new laws or by any kind of violence. And fourth, they would firmly reject the Aryan Paragraph.

On September 9, Bonhoeffer wrote Barth, asking whether this was the time for a *status confessionis*: "Several of us are now very drawn to the idea of the Free Church." He meant that they were willing to split from the German church. But Barth was convinced that they must not be the ones to leave; he said that they must wait until they were thrown out. "If there is schism," Barth wrote, "it must come from the other side." He even said that they must wait until there was a "clash over an even more central point."

Bonhoeffer and Hildebrandt wondered, *What could be more central than the Aryan Paragraph?* Bonhoeffer was so disturbed by Barth's response that he did not write him about the decision to go to London.

Niemöller sent "To the National Synod" to pastors across Germany. Much to the surprise of Bonhoeffer, Hildebrandt, and all involved, the response to the statement was extremely positive. The pastors across Germany who had signed this statement became an official organization: the Pastors' Emergency League. By the end of the year, six thousand pastors had become members. It was a major first step toward what would soon come to be known as the Confessing Church.

The German Christians Overreach

It was a heady time for the Nazis. The German Christians decided to celebrate their Reichsbischof victory by staging a massive rally in their favorite arena, the Berlin *Sportpalast*. The great hall was festooned with Nazi flags and banners declaring "One Reich. One People. One Church." Twenty thousand gathered to hear the leader of the Berlin German Christians, a high-school teacher named Reinhold Krause. This was his moment in the sun, and he seized it. But he seems to have leaped to the national stage with such eagerness that he hurt himself—and the German Christians—very badly.

Unaware that his speech would be heard beyond the devoted audience in the *Sportpalast* that day, Krause let fly with what he and the more passionate figures in the German Christian movement had been saying among themselves all along—but had not yet said publicly. The moderate mask they had presented to most Germans would now be taken off.

In coarse, crude language, Krause demanded that the German church must once and for all divest itself of every hint of Jewishness. The Old Testament would be first, "with its Jewish money morality and its tales of cattle merchants and pimps!" The stenographical record notes that "sustained applause" ensued. The New Testament must be revised, too, and must present a Jesus "corresponding entirely with the demands of National Socialism." And it must no longer present an "*exaggerated* emphasis on the crucified Christ." This tenet was defeatist and depressing, which was to say Jewish. Germany needed hope and victory! Krause also mocked "the theology of the Rabbi Paul with its scapegoats and inferiority complex," and then he mocked the symbol of the cross, "a ridiculous, debilitating remnant of Judaism, unacceptable to National Socialists!" Furthermore, he demanded that every German pastor must take an oath of personal allegiance to Hitler! And the Aryan Paragraph that demanded the expulsion of every church member of Jewish descent must be heartily accepted by every German church!

Krause gave the performance of his life, but it was a fatal miscalculation for the German Christians. In the morning the press reported that most Germans beyond the packed *Sportpalast* were outraged.

From that moment, the German Christian movement was effectively doomed. Mainstream Protestants saw them as beyond the pale, openly heretical, and fanatically Nazi. Most of the Nazis, who were not Christians at all, simply thought of them as laughable.

The London Pastorate

In October, Bonhoeffer turned his attention to London. His pastorate was to begin in two weeks, but Heckel made it clear that, given his recent activities, he might not be allowed to go. Bonhoeffer told Heckel he would recant nothing he had said or written. Nor would he promise to refrain from "ecumenical" activities while he was in London, as Heckel tried to get him to do. In the meeting with Heckel, Bonhoeffer even went so far as to demand a meeting with Reichsbischof Müller.

He met with Müller on October 4. He explained that he would not represent the German Christian Reichskirche in England and reiterated what he had told Heckel, that he would continue speaking to the ecumenical movement. When the semi-educated Müller asked him to recant his signature on the Pastors' Emergency League statement, he answered that he would not, and quoted the Augsburg Confession in Latin at great length. Müller grew uncomfortable and cut him off. In the end, fearing Bonhoeffer would cause more trouble if prevented, Müller let him go to London.

Karl Barth's apparent rebuff—on whether the approval of the Aryan Paragraph at the Brown Synod constituted a *status confessionis*—had been difficult to digest. On October 24, a week or so after he arrived, Bonhoeffer finally wrote Barth to tell him he had gone to London:

> If one were going to discover quite definite reasons for such decisions after the event, one of the strongest, I believe, was that I simply did not any longer feel up to the questions and

demands that came to me. I feel that, in some way I don't understand, I find myself in radical opposition to all my friends; I became increasingly isolated with my views of things, even though I was and remain personally close to these people. All this has frightened me and shaken my confidence so that I began to fear that dogmatism might be leading me astray— since there seemed no particular reason why my own view in these matters should be any better, any more right, than the views of many really capable pastors whom I sincerely respect.[3]

On November 20 came Barth's reply:

Dear Colleague!

You can deduce from the very way in which I address you that I do not regard your departure for England as anything but a necessary personal interlude. Once you had this thing on your mind, you were quite right not to ask for my wise counsel first. I would have advised you against it absolutely, and probably by bringing up my heaviest artillery. And now, as you are mentioning the matter to me after the fact, I can honestly not tell you anything but "Hurry back to your post in Berlin!" . . . With your splendid theological armor and your upright German figure, should you not perhaps be almost a little ashamed at a man like Heinrich Vogel, who, wizened and worked up as he is, is just always there, waving his arms like a windmill and shouting "Confession! Confession!" in his own way—in power or in weakness, that doesn't matter so much—actually giving his testimony? . . . Be glad that I do not have you here in person, for I would let go at you urgently in quite a different way, with the demand that you must not let go of all these intellectual flourishes and special consider-ations, however interesting they may be, and think of only one thing—that you are a German, that the house of your church is on fire, that you know enough and can say what you know well enough to be able to help, and that you must return to your post by the next ship. Given the situation, shall we say the ship after next? . . . Please take it [this letter] in the friendly spirit in which it is intended. If I were not so attached to you, I would not let fly at you in this way.

With sincere greetings,
Karl Barth[4]

In London that fall, Bonhoeffer met George Bell, bishop of Chichester, who would figure prominently in his life from that point forward. Bell and Bonhoeffer shared a February 4 birthday, although Bell was born in 1883. To his friends such as Franz Hildebrandt, Bonhoeffer would soon affectionately refer to Bell as Uncle George, though never to his face.

Bell was an impressive character. While dean of Canterbury, Bell had invited Dorothy Sayers and Christopher Fry as guest artists. But his most important invitation would be in 1935, when he commissioned T. S. Eliot to write the play *Murder in the Cathedral*, which dramatized the murder of Thomas à Becket that had taken place there in 1170. The play was an obvious criticism of the Nazi regime and premiered in the eponymous cathedral on June 15, 1935.

Bonhoeffer managed to keep closely involved in the Sturm und Drang of the church struggle. He traveled to Berlin every few weeks, and when he wasn't visiting Berlin, he was on the phone with someone there, whether Gerhard Jacobi, Martin Niemöller, or his mother, who was as immersed in the church struggle as anyone else. She fed her son every tidbit of information she gathered.

Hildebrandt arrived in London on November 10. He lived with Bonhoeffer in the parsonage for three months. People were constantly visiting. Everyone marveled at how Bonhoeffer and Hildebrandt lived "in a state of permanent dispute" that was somehow never acrimonious. They obviously enjoyed the constant theological bickering.

Bonhoeffer was responsible for two congregations, neither of which was large enough to support its own pastor. These expatriate congregations in London were similar to the expatriate congregation he had served in Barcelona. As with most ethnic communities abroad, the churches were the main cultural connection to the homeland. Also as in Barcelona, Bonhoeffer's sermons were strong meat for parishioners used to much lighter fare. In fact, they were now more demanding and severe than those he had preached five years earlier. He had changed much from the twenty-two-year-old in Barcelona; the circumstances had also obviously grown darker.

If Heckel and Müller thought letting Bonhoeffer go to London might mollify him somewhat or might keep him at arm's length from Berlin, they were mistaken. In London, Bonhoeffer was five times the trouble for them than he ever could have been back home. London gave Bonhoeffer a freedom he didn't have in Berlin, and he used it well. He deepened his relationships in the ecumenical world, and he made sure that whatever positive image Hitler's Germany might have in the English press was quickly corrected with facts.

The Church Battle Heats Up

In mid-November 1933, following the German Christians' fiasco at the Berlin *Sportpalast*, the forces that had opposed the German Christians clamored for Müller's resignation. He was scheduled to be consecrated on December 3 all the same. What's more, the Reichskirche invited the German pastors in England to come home to attend the ceremony.

Bonhoeffer had other ideas. First he tried to convince all the German pastors in England to stay away from the sham ceremony, and he succeeded with many of them. He persuaded those going to use the opportunity to deliver a document detailing their objections to Ludwig Müller. Titled "To the Reichskircharleitung," it catalogued the absurd statements and actions of Müller over the last few months. They could get their free trip home and still register an official and detailed protest. Müller's consecration ceremony was eventually postponed, so the document was not delivered personally, but it was sent to the leaders of the Reichskirche nonetheless.

As a result of the outcry over the *Sportpalast* event, the German Christians were in an awful position and losing ground by the hour. Müller executed a shocking about-face and rescinded the Aryan Paragraph. Bonhoeffer did not believe for a moment that any recent gains were permanent, and they weren't.

In early January, Müller spun back around and bared his teeth again, rescinding his previous rescindment: the Aryan Paragraph was suddenly back on. Before he did this, though, he gave himself some cover. On January 4 of the new year, he enacted what came to be known as the "muzzling decree." This decree declared that discussions concerning the church struggle could not take place in church buildings or be conducted in church newspapers. Anyone who did so would be dismissed. He further announced that all German church youth groups, called the Evangelical Youth, were to be merged with the Hitler Youth.

This was tantamount to a declaration of war. Bonhoeffer knew that because they could threaten to leave the Reichskirche, the German congregations abroad had leverage that the churches inside Germany did not. On Sunday, January 7, the German pastors sent a telegram to the Reichskirche: "For the sake of the Gospel and our conscience we associate ourselves with [the] Emergency League proclamation and withdraw our confidence from Reichsbischof Müller." On Monday the eighth, the Pastors' Emergency League planned to kick off its protest with a service at the magnificent and hugely important Berlin Cathedral, just across from the former kaiser's palace.

Müller caught wind of their plans and decided to head them off at the pass by obtaining a police order to keep the massive doors shut. But even Müller could not prevent the aggrieved faithful from gathering in the vast plaza outside the cathedral, which they did, and there they sang Luther's *"Ein Feste Burg."*[*] The gloves had come off.

On Thursday the eleventh, in an effort to lend some civility to the escalating ugliness, the aged Paul von Hindenburg shuffled into the fray and summoned Reichsbischof Müller to a meeting. Now eighty-six and only months from death, the titular president of the Reich represented a living, wheezing link with Germany's glorious past under the kaiser. On the twelfth, Hindenburg met with three members of the Pastors' Emergency League. On the thirteenth came the declaration of peace. The opposition pastors retracted their imminent threat to secede from the Reichskirche—but only for the time being.

On January 17, both sides were to meet with the Reichskanzler, Adolf Hitler. In early 1934, many in the Confessing Church, including Niemöller, still thought of Hitler as the reasonable one in all this, the man who would settle things in their favor. They were sure the smaller-minded men below him were to blame: it was Reichsbischof Müller who was Nazifying the church, not Hitler—and when they could finally meet with the chancellor, all would be clarified.

But Hitler postponed the meeting. Then postponed it again, till the twenty-fifth. The days of additional waiting were an eternity of strained inaction.

During this tense time in limbo, Bonhoeffer preached his now rather famous sermon on the prophet Jeremiah. It was Sunday, January 21. Preaching on a Jewish Old Testament prophet was quite out of the ordinary and provocative, but that was the least of the sermon's difficulties. The opening words were typically intriguing: "Jeremiah was not eager to become a prophet of God. When the call came to him all of a sudden, he shrank back, he resisted, he tried to get away."

---

* The hymn "A Mighty Fortress Is Our God."

The sermon reflected Bonhoeffer's own difficult situation. It is extremely doubtful whether anyone in his congregations could understand what he was talking about, much less accept that it was God's word to them that Sunday. If they had ever been puzzled by their brilliant young preacher's homilies, they must have been puzzled now.

Meeting with Hitler and Meeting with Heckel

Finally January 25 came, and both sides met with Adolf Hitler. It did not go well for the opposition in general, but it was Niemöller, up to this point their most pro-Nazi figure, who got the worst of it.

Göring had had Niemöller's telephone tapped, and he opened the long-awaited meeting by producing the transcript of a call in which Niemöller had spoken ill of Hindenburg's influence on Hitler. Hitler was not amused. "This is completely unheard of!" he fumed. "I will attack this rebellion with every means at my disposal!"

"I was very frightened," Niemöller said later. "I thought, what do I answer to all his complaints and accusations? [Hitler] was still speaking, speaking, speaking. I thought, dear God, let him stop." In an attempt to put a better face on things, Niemöller declared truthfully, "But we are all enthusiastic about the Third Reich." Hitler exploded. "I'm the one who built the Third Reich!" he fumed. "You just worry about your sermons!" In that painful, sobering moment, Niemöller's fantasy that the Third Reich was a legitimate movement was dashed. He now saw that the only principles of the Third Reich were the desires and will of the man ranting in front of him.

Bonhoeffer preached twice on his birthday, February 4, as he did every Sunday, but in the evening he gathered with a few friends and got a phone call from 14 Wangenheimstrasse, where the whole family had gathered just to wish him a happy birthday. One of the letters he had received that day was from his father, who revealed something he had never said to his son before:

Dear Dietrich,

At the time when you decided to study theology, I sometimes thought to myself that a quiet, uneventful pastor's life,
as I knew it from that of my Swabian uncle . . . would really
almost be a pity for you. So far as uneventfulness is concerned, I was greatly mistaken. That such a crisis should still
be possible in the ecclesiastical field seemed to me, with my
scientific background, to be out of the question. But in this as
in many other things, it appears that we older folks have had
quite wrong ideas about the solidity of so-called established
concepts, views, and things. . . . In any case, you gain one
thing from your calling—and in this it resembles mine—living
relationships to human beings and the possibility of meaning
something to them, in more important matters than medical
ones. And of this nothing can be taken away from you, even
when the external institutions in which you are placed are not
always as you would wish.[5]

A tense and unproductive series of meetings with Heckel followed in London. Finally, an irate and flustered Heckel summoned
Bonhoeffer to Berlin for a dressing-down. Bonhoeffer arrived on
March 5. When he met with Heckel this time, the newly minted
bishop did not mince words: Bonhoeffer must henceforth refrain
from all ecumenical activity. Bonhoeffer refused.

The Confessing Church
on the Banks of the Rubicon

While in Berlin, Bonhoeffer met with Martin Niemöller, Gerhard
Jacobi, and other leaders in the Pastors' Emergency League. Their
moment of truth had arrived. They agreed this was the *status confessionis* that Bonhoeffer had been saying it was all along, and they
would hold the synod for a Free Church in Barmen at the end

of May. It would be a watershed event and would officially and publicly separate them from the apostate Reichskirche. They had come to the banks of the Rubicon and were girding themselves for the crossing.

In the midst of a whirlwind of ecumenical activity, Bonhoeffer continued to serve as the main pastor for two congregations, preaching twice each Sunday and carrying out his innumerable functions as a pastor. On April 12 he learned that Müller had nominated as *Rechtswalter* (legal administrator) over the German church a racist fanatic named Dr. August Jäger. In a speech the year before, Jäger had wackily declared, "The appearance of Jesus in world history ultimately represents a burst of Nordic light in the midst of a world tormented by symptoms of degeneracy."

On April 15, Bonhoeffer wrote Bishop Bell:

> The appointment of Dr. Jäger . . . is an ostentatious affront to the opposition and . . . means in fact that all power of the church government has been handed over to political and party authorities. It was much surprising to me that the *Times* gave a rather positive report to this appointment. Jäger is in fact the man with the famous statement about Jesus being only the exponent of Nordic race etc. He was the man who caused the retirement of Bodelschwingh and who was considered to be the most ruthless man in the whole church government. . . . So this appointment must be taken as a significant step towards the complete assimilation of the church to the state and party. Even if Jäger should try to make himself sympathetic to the churches abroad, by using mild words now, one must not be deceived by this tactic.[6]

On the last three days of May 1934, the leaders of the Pastors' Emergency League held the synod in Barmen. It was there, on the Wupper River, that they wrote the famous Barmen Declaration, from which emerged what came to be known as the Confessing Church.*

The purpose of the Barmen Declaration was to state what the German church had always believed, to ground it in the Scriptures, and to differentiate it from the bastardized theology that had been coming from the German Christians. The principal author of the Barmen Confession was Karl Barth, who claimed to have produced the final version "fortified by strong coffee and one or two Brazilian cigars."

Martin Niemöller (left) and Rev. Otto Dibelius (right) flank the Bishop of Chichester, George Bell.

(AP Images)

On June 4—thanks to Bishop Bell and Bonhoeffer—the full text of the Barmen Declaration was published in the London *Times*. It was

---

* The term *confess* means "to give assent to" or "to acknowledge." It echoes Jesus' statement from the gospel of Matthew that "whoever confesses Me before men, him I will also confess before My Father who is in heaven" (10:32 NKJV). At first some called it the Confessional Movement. The German term for "Confessional Church" was *Bekennende Kirche*, so it is sometimes abbreviated BK.

incendiary, announcing to the world that a group of Christians in Germany had officially and publicly declared their independence from the Nazified Reichskirche. When one read it, it was easy to understand why they had done so.

As Bonhoeffer took great pains to make clear, the Barmen Declaration did not constitute a secession from the "official" German church; calling it a secession would give an appearance of legitimacy to that "official" German church. But not everyone saw this as clearly as Bonhoeffer had expected.

Bonhoeffer had been asked to give a speech at the ecumenical conference in Fanø, Denmark, that August and to organize the youth conference that was part of the larger conference, but he soon discovered that some German delegates invited to the Fanø conference were part of the Reichskirche led by Müller. Bonhoeffer immediately contacted the Fanø organizers, making his position clear: if Heckel and the Reichskirche were there, they would be there alone. The silence of the Confessing Church would speak for itself.

This would soon get awkward: an invitation had already been extended to Heckel and the Reichskirche's Foreign Office. Bonhoeffer was exasperated. On July 12, Bonhoeffer wrote the organizers:

> There is not the claim or even the wish to be a Free Church beside the *Reichskirche*, but there is the claim to be the only theologically and legally legitimate evangelical church in Germany . . .[7]

The Night of the Long Knives

During that summer of 1934, dramatic changes were taking place in Germany. Taken together, they powerfully altered the political landscape, which would have a direct bearing on everyone's future for years to come and would immediately affect who would attend the ecumenical conference at Fanø.

Bonhoeffer heard from his brother-in-law Dohnanyi that Hjalmar Schacht, the head of the German *Reichsbank*, was on the verge of resigning. Then President Hindenburg's doctors leaked the news that he was likely only months from death. Hitler feared that as soon as Hindenburg died, the conservatives and the army leaders would push hard for a return to the monarchy. But having sniffed the political winds with canine sensitivity, he bound ahead of the situation, and with lupine ruthlessness, he ordered a savage blood-bath that came to be known as the *Nacht der Langen Messer* (Night of the Long Knives).*

On June 29, an extraordinary murder spree was unleashed, a ghastly tableau of bloodletting across Germany in which hundreds of people were slain in cold blood. Some were dragged out of bed and shot in their homes; some were killed by firing squads; others were sent to eternity sitting at their desks; wives were dispatched with their husbands; and ancient enemies from the failed putsch of 1923 were avenged, one with pickaxes. SA leader Ernst Röhm was awakened in his hotel room, dressed down personally by an irate Hitler, and then hauled off to a prison cell in Munich, where he was suggestively sequestered with a loaded revolver.

When it was all over, Hitler claimed that a Röhm putsch had been imminent, but with the help of Providence it had been avoided. In later years the figure was put at 400 or even 1,000 people mur-dered. As usual, Hitler raged that he had been provoked to his actions—that a coup was in the works, that indeed his own life had been threatened, and that these murders were in the best interests of the German *Volk*, for whom no sacrifice was too great!

On July 13, Hitler gave a speech to the Reichstag:

If anyone reproaches me and asks why I did not resort to the regular courts of justice, then all I can say is this: In this hour I

---

* Absurdly, it was also referred to as Operation Hummingbird.

was responsible for the fate of the German people, and thereby I
became the supreme judge of the German people. . . . Everyone
must know for all future time that if he raises his hand to strike
the State, then certain death is his lot.[8]

It all had a chilling effect on most Germans. Bonhoeffer's student Inge Karding recalled the mood that followed this episode: "A
crippling fear rose up like a bad odor within you."

Three weeks later, Hindenburg died. When the war hero gave
up the ghost on August 2 at the age of eighty-six, Hitler—lickety-
split—announced his choice for Hindenburg's replacement. He
himself would be Hindenburg's successor! He would remain chancellor as well. The two offices of president and chancellor would be
combined in one person, as this was the will of the German people.
A plebiscite was announced for later that month. As one might have
foreseen, 90 percent of the German people voted *Ja*.

Playing on the deeply patriotic mood that attended Hindenburg's
death, Hitler summoned the military officers and troops of the Berlin
garrison to the Königsplatz where, by flickering torchlight, they
renewed their oath of allegiance. But when their hands were raised,
they found themselves swearing an oath that was not what they had
expected. It was not an oath to the German constitution or to the
German nation, but to the fellow with the mustache. According to
what they were swearing, Hitler had become the living embodiment of German will and law. The oath came quite to the point: "I
swear by God this sacred oath, that I will render unconditional obedience to Adolf Hitler, the Führer of the German Reich and people,
Supreme Commander of the Armed Forces, and will be ready as a
brave soldier to risk my life at any time for this oath."

They pronounced these words en masse, frozen in their forma-
tions and unable to scratch their heads at what had just happened.
They had been magnificently snookered. Germans in general, and
military men in particular, took obedience and oaths extremely

seriously, and these few words, assented to under some duress, would pay handsome dividends for the Führer in the years ahead. The German people found themselves far from shore, alone in a boat with a madman.

CHAPTER 7

ZINGST AND FINKENWALDE

1935–1937

Only he who cries out for the Jews may sing Gregorian chants.

—DIETRICH BONHOEFFER

ltimately, Bonhoeffer made it to Fanø, and the radical nature of what he said and did there is difficult to over-state. His hope that the youth conference would result in some bold and substantive resolutions was not disappointed. The fifty delegates drew up two resolutions. The first said that God's commandments utterly trumped any claims of the state. It passed narrowly, with many of Bonhoeffer's Berlin students registering contrary votes. The second condemned Christian support for "any war whatsoever." A Polish delegate suggested emending it to a condemnation of "aggressive war" rather than "any war whatsoever," but that was not accepted by the others. There was a lively debate on conscientious objection, which spilled out, as all the larger scheduled discussions did, into smaller conversations among the participants. The German students were brave to discuss such things at all.

During the days, Bonhoeffer and the youth conference participants gathered on the Fanø beaches for informal discussions. During one seaside conversation, a Swede asked Bonhoeffer what he would do if war came. According to those present, Bonhoeffer quietly scooped up a handful of sand and let it run out between his fingers as he pondered the question and his answer. Then looking calmly at the young man, he replied, "I pray that God will give me the strength then not to take up a weapon."

Bonhoeffer had known Dr. Henry Smith Leiper at Union. In Fanø, Bonhoeffer went to Leiper's room to talk, telling him of the situation with Heckel and how Heckel had informed him that he must leave London. Leiper recalled their conversation:

> When I asked what his reply had been to the Bishop's order, he said with a grim smile: "Negative." Amplifying that laconic remark he said: "I told him he would have to come to London to get me if he wanted me out of that church." With utter candor and fearless scorn he talked of what the followers of Christ must be prepared to do in resisting Nazi Caesarism and its penetration of spiritual domains. From that it was quite plain to me that he was prepared to fight the régime of Ludwig Müller. Yet at no point in our conversation did he show any concern for what might be the consequences of his decision to oppose openly the whole effort of Hitlerism to take over the control of the Church in Germany. Nor did he show the least doubt that the discerning Christians would have to deal realistically with the most dangerous and unscrupulous dictator who believed that he could achieve his plan for making what he called "practical Christianity" a source of power and influence for his political platform.

It was very significant that Dietrich should have had such

clear insights and could have reached such bold decisions so early in the official life of Hitler's thrust into the administrative life of the churches. From my own somewhat extensive experience in many earlier visits to Germany I knew that hardly any of his colleagues were as wise and fearless as he with respect to what was afoot. Nor were many of them as defiant—at least openly—towards the tyranny which had loomed on the horizons of their country in the "miracle" of the Third Reich. . . . Dietrich was determined to approach the problems raised by the Nazi movement not merely from a theological or philosophical point of view but with directness of action.[1]

The resolution at Fanø was the united voice of a great multitude from around the world:

The Council declares its conviction that autocratic Church rule, especially when imposed upon the conscience in solemn oath, the use of force, and the suppression of free discussion, are incompatible with the true nature of the Christian Church, and asks in the name of the Gospel for its fellow Christians in the German Church:

"Freedom to preach the Gospel of our Lord Jesus Christ and to live according to His teaching;

"Freedom of the printed word and of Assembly in the service of the Christian Community;

"Freedom for the Church to instruct its youth in the principles of Christianity and immunity from the compulsory imposition of a philosophy of life antagonistic to the Christian religion."[2]

On the morning of the twenty-eighth, Bonhoeffer gave his memorable "Peace Speech" to the assembly. "From the first moment," said Otto Dudzus, one of his students from Berlin, "the assembly was breathless with tension. Many may have felt that they would never forget what they had just heard." The twenty-eight-year-old Bonhoeffer's words from that morning are still quoted:

> There is no way to peace along the way of safety. For peace must be dared, it is itself the great venture and can never be safe. Peace is the opposite of security. To demand guarantees is to want to protect oneself. Peace means giving oneself completely to God's commandment, wanting no security, but in faith and obedience laying the destiny of the nations in the hand of Almighty God, not trying to direct it for selfish purposes. Battles are won, not with weapons, but with God. They are won when the way leads to the cross.[3]

One student recalled that Bonhoeffer's last sentences were unforgettable: "What are we waiting for? The time is late." After Bonhoeffer finished, the leader of the conference came to the podium and stated that it wasn't necessary to comment on the speech; its meaning had been clear to everyone.

Meanwhile, Barth was attempting to meet with Hitler. Many in the Confessing Church still thought Hitler might be reasoned with. Bonhoeffer had already seen through this. In his letter to Sutz, he referred to Barth's idea:

> From now on, I believe, any discussion between Hitler and Barth would be quite pointless—indeed, no longer to be sanctioned. Hitler has shown himself quite plainly for what he is, and the church ought to know with whom it has to reckon. Isaiah didn't go to Sennacherib either. We have tried often enough—too often—to make Hitler aware of what is going on. Maybe we've not yet gone about it in the right way, but then Barth won't go about it the right way either. Hitler is not in a position to listen to us; he is *obdurate*, and as such he must

compel *us* to listen—it's that way round. The Oxford movement was naïve enough to try and convert Hitler—a ridiculous failure to recognize what is going on. *We* are the ones to be converted, not Hitler.[4]

Zingst

On October 19 the members of the Confessing Church convened in Dahlem, issuing the famous Dahlem Resolution: "We call upon the Christian congregations, their pastors and elders, to ignore any instructions received from the former Reichskirche government and its authorities and to refrain from cooperating with those who wish to continue to obey that same church government. We call upon them to adhere to the directions of the Confessional synod of the German Evangelical Church and its recognized bodies."

No one could say they weren't an official church anymore. Bonhoeffer was quite pleased. The synod also enacted a resolution accusing Müller of violating the constitution of the German Evangelical Church. Bonhoeffer heard from his brother-in-law Dohnanyi that as a result of these very public troubles, Hitler had begun to turn his attention to the church struggle. Things had to be formalized, so copies of the resolution were sent to Heckel in the Foreign Office and to Karl Koch at the Confessing Synod, and a letter was enclosed:

> The German Evangelical congregations in Great Britain have heard with great pleasure that, as a result of the Führer's declarations, the conscious profession of loyalty to the Third Reich and its Führer is not identical with membership in any one church group. These congregations have been based, some of them for centuries, upon the Bible and the Confession, and therefore consider the Confessional church to be the rightful successor of the German Evangelical Church Federation.[5]

Earlier in the year, the leaders of the Confessing Church had realized that they must think about opening their own seminaries. The Reichskirche required that all university theological students prove their Aryan racial purity. Jacobi and Hildebrandt had suggested that Bonhoeffer run a Confessing Church seminary, but if Bonhoeffer wanted to continue his studies at the University of Berlin, he needed to decide soon; his leave of absence could not last forever. Finally he made his decision. In mid-January, he wrote his eldest brother to tell him about choosing to lead an illegal Confessing Church seminary.

He preached his last sermons in London on March 10, and shortly afterward he left for a tour of British Christian communities. On April 15, he left London for Berlin, to report for duty as the imminent head of the first seminary in the Confessing Church. Twenty-three ordinands were ready, but there was still no place to house them, although many of them had already arrived in Berlin.

On April 25, Bonhoeffer received word that the Rhineland Bible School in Zingst on the Baltic coast was available until June 14. Until one day in 1874, Zingst was an island in the Baltic Sea. Then a storm created a hundred-yard-wide land bridge to the Pomeranian coast, overnight transforming the island into a peninsula, which it has remained. It was to that young peninsula that Bonhoeffer and his ordinands traveled, at the end of April 1935, with the plan of opening a seminary in the brand-new Confessing Church.

The ramshackle retreat center, intended for summer use, lay just behind the dunes and beach, which at that time of the year could be brutally cold and windy. But there were a half-timbered farmhouse and a number of unheated thatched cottages where the ordinands could live. Everyone was young and up for an adventure, including Bonhoeffer. The next day Bonhoeffer led his flock of ordinands two hundred miles north to the sea, there to inaugurate the experiment in Christian living he had been dreaming about.

Bonhoeffer had in mind a kind of monastic community, where one aimed to live in the way Jesus commanded his followers to live in his Sermon on the Mount, where one lived not merely as a theological student but as a disciple of Christ. It would be an unorthodox experiment in communal Christian living, in the "life together," as Bonhoeffer would so famously put it.

No one in the Lutheran tradition had ever tried such a thing. The knee-jerk reaction away from anything that smacked of Roman Catholicism was strong, but Bonhoeffer had long before moved past parochialism and was willing to bear such criticisms. He felt that Lutheran Christianity had slid away from Luther's intentions, just as Luther felt that the Roman Catholic Church had moved away from St. Peter's and, more importantly, from Christ's.

Bonhoeffer (right) and Eberhard Bethge during the summer of 1938, in the parish house at Gross-Schlönwitz.

(Art Resource, NY)

Four of the twenty-three ordinands came from Saxony, Eberhard Bethge among them. Bethge arrived on one of the last days of April, just after the evening meal. He immediately ran out to the beach, where everyone was playing soccer, as they often did at that part of the day. He asked where *Herr Direktor* was. They pointed out Bonhoeffer. Bethge had never heard of him before and knew nothing of his leadership in the church struggle. He was surprised at how young and athletic Bonhoeffer looked, and at first he found it impossible to differentiate him from the students.

When Bonhoeffer finally realized that another ordinand had arrived, he left what he was doing, greeted Bethge, and invited him to take a walk along the beach. Neither young man could imagine how important their meeting would seem later. Bonhoeffer asked Bethge about his family and upbringing, his expulsion by Reichsbischof Müller, and his experiences in the church struggle.

The two men soon saw that they were more in tune with each other than anyone else in their lives. Each had extraordinary intellectual and aesthetic sensibilities in literature, art, and music. They would soon become such close friends that many of the other ordinands grew jealous of their relationship. They had no inkling that their friendship, not yet begun, would become the means by which Bonhoeffer's writings were preserved and disseminated throughout the world for generations.

Finkenwalde

The humble accommodations at Zingst had to be vacated by June 14, and a more permanent home found as soon as possible. They considered a number of properties, but finally settled on the former von Katte estate in Finkenwalde, a small town not far from Stettin in Pomerania. Bonhoeffer inaugurated Finkenwalde with his first lecture there on June 26.

The landed gentry of Pomerania were strongly against Hitler

and the Nazis, and they were generally devout Christians too. Many of these families practically adopted the Finkenwaldians as their personal project, wanting to help the brave, fledgling enterprise however they could. One day the phone rang and the ordinands learned that someone had sent Pastor Bonhoeffer a live pig. It was at the local freight yard, waiting to be picked up. Bonhoeffer himself donated his entire theological library, including his great-grandfather von Hase's invaluable Erlangen edition of Martin Luther's works. He brought his gramophone, too, and his many recordings, the most prized and exotic of which remained the Negro spirituals he had bought in Manhattan.

At Zingst and Finkenwalde, Bonhoeffer emphasized a strict daily routine and the spiritual disciplines. That aspect of the seminary most resembled what Bonhoeffer had found at the English Christian communities he had visited. But the specifics of what filled the daily routine were of his own devising and borrowed from many traditions.

Each day began with a forty-five-minute service before breakfast and ended with a service just before bed. One student from Finkenwalde, Albrecht Schönherr, recalled that the morning service began within minutes of waking:

> Bonhoeffer requested us not to say a single word to each other before the service. The first word to come was supposed to be God's word. But this was not so simple, because we spent all the time in a room in which we slept six or eight at a time, and we slept on old featherbeds, [on top of] hay mattresses. These mattresses had been used for generations. When you lay down on them, there was a huge dust explosion.[6]

The services took place not in the chapel, but around the large dinner table. They began by singing a choral psalm and a hymn chosen for that day. Then there was a reading from the Old Testament.

Next they sang "a set verse from a hymn," using the same verse for several weeks, followed by a New Testament reading.

One meditated on the same verse for an entire week, a half hour each day. Wolf-Dieter Zimmermann recalled that they were not allowed to look at the text in the original language or to consult reference books or commentaries. They must deal with the verse as though it was God's word to them personally. Many seminarians chafed at the practice, but it wasn't only ordinands who were bothered by the practice of meditation on Scripture verses. In a letter in October 1936, Karl Barth wrote that he was disturbed by what he described as

> an almost indefinable odor of a monastic eros and pathos. I can hardly say that I am very happy about it . . . . I cannot go with the distinction in principle between theological work and devotional edification. . . . Do not regard this as a criticism of your efforts simply because the basis of my knowledge and my understanding is still far too scanty. But you will at least understand from this the questions that I would put to you despite all my sympathies.

Bonhoeffer wrote Barth, partially in response to his concern about Finkenwalde's "monastic" atmosphere. Bonhoeffer himself was critical of "pietistic" communities, but he knew that regarding all emphasis on prayer and spiritual disciplines as "legalism" was equally erroneous.

Bonhoeffer also took preaching seriously. For him a sermon was nothing less than the very word of God, a place where God would speak to his people. Bonhoeffer wanted to impress this idea on his ordinands, to help them see that preaching was not merely an intellectual exercise. Like prayer or meditation on a scriptural text, it was an opportunity to hear from heaven, and for the preacher, it was a holy privilege to be the vessel through whom God would speak.

Bonhoeffer "always had some distance around him, some reserve," recalled one observer at this time. But there was something compelling about him when he was preaching. "When you saw him preaching," she said, "you saw a young man who was entirely in God's grasp. . . . In those days, the Nazis were always marching and saying, 'The future belongs to us! We are the future!' And we young ones who were against Hitler and the Nazis would hear this and we wondered, 'Where is our future?' But there in Finkenwalde, when I heard this man preaching, who had been captured by God, I thought: 'Here. Here is our future.'"

Once a month, on a Saturday evening, all the ordinands took part in a Communion service. One such Saturday before this service, Bonhoeffer broached the subject of personal confession between them. It had been Luther's idea that Christians should confess to one another instead of to a priest. Most Lutherans had thrown that baby out with the bathwater and didn't confess to anyone. Confession of any kind was considered overly Catholic, just as extemporaneous prayer was criticized as too pietistic. But Bonhoeffer successfully instituted the practice of confessing one to another. Perhaps not surprisingly, Bonhoeffer chose Eberhard Bethge as his confessor.

The Nuremberg Laws

On September 15, 1935, the Nuremberg Laws were announced. These "Laws for the Protection of German Blood and German Honor" stated:

> Entirely convinced that the purity of German blood is essential to the further existence of the German people, and inspired by the uncompromising determination to safeguard the future of the German nation, the Reichstag has unanimously resolved upon the following law, which is promulgated herewith:
> Section 1 1. Marriages between Jews and citizens of German or kindred blood are forbidden. Marriages

concluded in defiance of this law are void, even if, for the purpose of evading this law, they were concluded abroad. 2. Proceedings for annulment may be initiated only by the Public Prosecutor.

Section 2 1. Extramarital intercourse between Jews and subjects of the state of Germany or related blood is forbidden.

Section 3 Jews will not be permitted to employ female citizens of German or kindred blood as domestic workers under the age of 45.

Section 4 1. Jews are forbidden to display the Reichsflagge or the national colors. 2. On the other hand they are permitted to display the Jewish colors. The exercise of this right is protected by the State.[7]

The Nuremberg Laws represented what has been called a second, "more ordered" phase of Jewish persecution. Jews, who were once legal citizens of Germany, were becoming subjects of the Third Reich. Bonhoeffer had known of this pending legislation through Dohnanyi, who had tried to thwart it, or blunt it, in vain.

Bonhoeffer saw the enactment of these laws as an opportunity for the Confessing Church to speak out clearly, in a way they had not yet been able to do. The Nazis had drawn a line in the sand and everyone could see it. Bonhoeffer believed it was the role of the church to *speak for those who could not speak.* Around this time, he made his famous declaration: "Only he who cries out for the Jews may sing Gregorian chants."

But the Confessing Church was again slow to act. It was guilty of the typically Lutheran error of confining itself to the narrow sphere of how church and state were related. One day, from his home church in Dahlem, Franz Hildebrandt called Finkenwalde with alarming news. The Confessing Synod was proposing a resolution conceding the state's right to enact the Nuremberg legislation. It was the last straw for him. Hildebrandt was ready to resign from the Pastors' Emergency

League and to leave the Confessing Church. Bonhoeffer decided he must do something, so he and a group of ordinands went to Berlin to see whether they might influence things at the synod, which would be held in Steglitz.

The synod did not approve the resolution, but it also failed to take a stand. The National Socialists' strategy of dividing and conquering its opponents, of confusing and delaying, was working with the Confessing Church.

Between Scylla and Charybdis

On February 4, 1936, Bonhoeffer celebrated his thirtieth birthday. He had always felt overly conscious of his age and thought thirty impossibly old. It was the last such milestone he would see. And it was the celebration of this birthday that would for the first time bring him into the sights of the Nazis.

It began innocently enough in one of the many postprandial conversations with his ordinands in the main hall at Finkenwalde. They had been celebrating Bonhoeffer's birthday in the usual manner, with singing and other tributes to the honoree, and when the evening was winding down, they got into a rather freewheeling conversation about gift giving. Someone brightly suggested that perhaps the person celebrating a birthday should not be the one to receive the gifts but to give them—and his friends should be the recipients. When Bonhoeffer took the bait and inquired what everyone might want, they settled on the idea of a trip to Sweden. Would he organize one for them? As it turned out, he would.

The trip to Sweden was one of many examples of Bonhoeffer's generosity. One ordinand at Gross-Schlönwitz, Hans-Werner Jensen, said that "serving his brothers became the center of Bonhoeffer's life. He avoided keeping them in tutelage; he only wanted to help them." Jensen recalled other incidents of Bonhoeffer's generosity. When Jensen was at Stolp hospital with appendicitis, he was transferred from the third-class ward to a private room. "The orderly told me that a good-looking gentleman with glasses had been in that morning declaring he would bear the cost. . . . Another time we were making our way home after an open evening in Berlin. Bonhoeffer bought the tickets for all of us at the station. When I wanted to repay him, he just answered: 'Money is dirt.'"

This was a grand opportunity to show his ordinands the church beyond Germany. He had captivated them many times with tales of his trips abroad. And he had explained that the church was something that transcended national boundaries, that it extended throughout time and space. There were many good reasons for such a trip, not least to afford his ordinands some measure of the culturally broadening experiences he'd had in spades. Bonhoeffer also knew strengthening Finkenwalde's ties to the ecumenical church abroad would be helpful in safeguarding it from Nazi interference.

On March 1, the ordinands and instructors boarded a ship in the port of Stettin and sailed northward to Sweden, unaware that Heckel and the Foreign Ministry had already taken an interest in their adventure.

Bonhoeffer knew the dangers of such a trip and had warned his ordinands to be very careful about what they said, especially to newspaper reporters. On March 3 the Swedish press put the seminarians' visit on their front pages, and the next day their visit to Archbishop Eidem in Uppsala made the papers too. On the sixth, in Stockholm, they called on the German ambassador, Prince Victor zu Wied. The prince, having just read a warning letter about this troublemaker, received Bonhoeffer and his associates with obvious coolness. Bonhoeffer didn't know why, but later recalled a life-sized portrait of Hitler in the room glowering at them.

With their arrival in Stockholm came many more articles and photographs. Each column inch of international coverage made Heckel look worse. He fired off a letter to the Swedish church. Next, he wrote a letter to the Prussian church committee, taking them to task. This time he brought out the big artillery, and blasted Bonhoeffer officially in writing and in terms that moved the whole dispute to another level:

> I feel impelled . . . to draw the attention of the provincial church committee to the fact that the incident has brought Bonhoeffer very much into the public eye. Since he can be accused of being a pacifist and an enemy of the state it might well be advisable for the provincial church committee to disassociate itself from him and to take steps to ensure that he will no longer train German theologians.[8]

A corner had been turned. Heckel had placed Bonhoeffer at the mercy of the Nazi state. Bethge wrote that "no form of denunciation was more fatal than the description 'a pacifist and an enemy of the state,' especially when this was used officially and in writing."

The immediate upshot was that Bonhoeffer's right to teach at Berlin University was officially revoked. He had given a lecture there on February 14, which turned out to be his last. His long relationship with the world of academia ended forever. His brother-in-law Gerhard Leibholz was forced to "retire" that April. In some ways the judgment was a badge of honor.

An Atrocious Piece of False Doctrine

On April 22, Bonhoeffer delivered a lecture titled "The Question of the Boundaries of the Church and Church Union." It was typically measured, thorough, and definitive, to the point of being elegant and beautiful, like a winning equation. But someplace in this beautiful landscape, planted like a time bomb, was a single devastating sentence. It would soon explode and cause a firestorm of controversy. The sentence was this: "Whoever knowingly separates himself from the Confessing Church in Germany separates himself from salvation."

The condemnations were thundering. When the lecture was published in the June issue of *Evangelische Theologie*, the paper quickly sold out. Bonhoeffer's essay led Hermann Sasse, who had cowritten the Bethel Confession with him, to declare that the Confessing Church as "distinct from the confessional movement upheld by the Lutheran churches, is a sect, the worst sect in fact ever to have set foot on the soil of German Protestantism." Someone called Bonhoeffer's declaration "the ecstatic effusion of a hitherto level-headed man, contradicting everything that was essential to Luther." General Superintendent Ernst Stoltenhoff called it "nothing more than an atrocious piece of false doctrine."

Bonhoeffer wrote to Erwin Sutz:

> My paper has made me the most reviled man of our persua-
> sion. . . . . Things are approaching the stage when the beast
> before which the idol worshippers bow down will bear the cari-
> cature of Luther's features. . . . Either the Barmen Declaration is a
> true confession of the Lord Jesus Christ which has been brought
> about through the Holy Spirit, in which case it can make or
> divide a church—or it is an unofficial expression of the opin-
> ion of a number of theologians, in which case the Confessing
> Church has been on the wrong track for a long time.[9]

That summer the Olympic Games afforded Hitler a singular opportunity to show the cheerful, reasonable face of the "new Germany." Goebbels, who spared no expense in building his cathedrals of deceit, erected a veritable Chartres of trickery and fraud.

The Nazis did their best to portray Germany as a Christian nation. The Reichskirche erected a huge tent near the Olympic stadium. Foreigners would have no idea of the internecine battle between the German Christians and the Confessing Church; it simply looked like there was an abundance of Christianity in the midst of Hitler's Germany.

At St. Paul's Church, the Confessing Church sponsored a series of lectures: Jacobi, Niemöller, and Bonhoeffer spoke. "Not a bad evening yesterday," Bonhoeffer wrote. "The church packed; people were sitting on the altar steps and standing everywhere. I wish I could have preached instead of giving a lecture." Most of the Confessing Church lectures were packed.

In the spring of 1937, Bonhoeffer wrote another dramatic paper titled "Statements about the Power of the Keys and Church Discipline in the New Testament." He was trying to get the church to take itself seriously, to grasp what power God had given it, an awesome and frightening power that needed to be understood and used as God intended. Just as he spoke to his ordinands about preaching the Word, he now spoke to the whole Confessing Church. The paper begins:

> 1. Christ has given his church power to forgive and to retain sins on earth with divine authority (Matt. 16:19; 18:18; John 20:23). Eternal salvation and eternal damnation are decided by its word. Anyone who turns from his sinful way at the word of proclamation and repents, receives forgiveness. Anyone who perseveres in his sin receives judgement. The church cannot loose the penitent from sin without arresting and binding the impenitent in sin.[10]

There was nothing wishy-washy about it. Later he touched on the concept of cheap grace—without using the term—and he commented on how the ecumenical movement and the Confessing Church had sometimes engaged in well-intentioned dialogue with Hitler and the Reichskirche:

> 3. "Do not give dogs what is holy; and do not throw your pearls before swine, lest they trample them underfoot and turn to attack you" (Matt. 7:6). The promise of grace is not to be squandered; it needs to be protected from the godless. There

are those who are not worthy of the sanctuary. The proclamation of grace has its limits. Grace may not be proclaimed to anyone who does not recognize or distinguish or desire it. Not only does that pollute the sanctuary itself, not only must those who sin still be guilty against the Most Holy, but in addition, the misuse of the Holy must turn against the community itself.[11]

The Nazis Crack Down

Even when trampling, the Nazis had been canny and careful to that point. They were exceedingly sensitive to public opinion, and their approach to the Confessing Church had been mostly one of ever-increasing and ever-tightening regulations. Their methods were "not so much aimed at banning the Confessing Church directly," Bethge said, "but gradually liquidating it through intimidation and the suppression of individual activities."

They forbade the reading of intercessory prayer lists from the pulpit and revoked passports; Niemöller's passport had been revoked earlier in the year. In June the Nazis declared that all collections taken during services of the Confessing Church were illegal. In July all "duplicate communication" would be subject to the Nazis' Editorial Law and would receive the same treatment as newspapers. The welter of inane regulations and unjust laws overwhelmed the Confessing pastors, who were constantly running afoul of one of them and being arrested.

But in 1937, the Nazis abandoned all pretense of being even-handed and came down hard on the Confessing Church. That year more than eight hundred Confessing Church pastors and lay leaders were imprisoned or arrested. The outspoken Martin Niemöller of Dahlem was among them. On June 27, he preached what would be his last sermon for many years. Crowds had overflowed his church week after week. That final Sunday, Niemöller was no less outspoken than he had always been. From the pulpit he declared, "We have no more thought of using our own powers to escape the arm of the authorities, than had the Apostles of old. No more are we ready to keep silent at man's behest when God commands us to speak. For it is, and must remain, the case that we must obey God rather than man." Bonhoeffer and Bethge were in Berlin that day. The arrests of the Confessing Church pastors had been increasing, so they went to Niemöller's house to strategize with him and Hildebrandt. But they found only Hildebrandt and Niemöller's wife. The Gestapo had arrested Niemöller just moments earlier.

The four of them were talking about what to do next when several black Mercedes pulled up to the house. Knowing these to be Gestapo, Bonhoeffer, Bethge, and Hildebrandt made for the back door and were there stopped by Herr Höhle, a Gestapo official already familiar to them and most of the Confessing Church. The three men were escorted back into the house, searched by another officer, and then placed under house arrest, where they remained for seven hours, during which time they sat and watched as the Niemöllers' house was searched. The Gestapo's meticulous perseverance was eventually rewarded with the discovery of a safe behind a picture, and the thousand marks within, belonging to the Pastors' Emergency League.

Niemöller's ten-year-old son, Jan, remembered that anyone who showed up at the house that day was detained and fell under suspicion. "The house became full," he said. Somehow the inimitable Paula Bonhoeffer got wind of the situation. Bonhoeffer saw his parents' car pass several times, his mother peeking out. Everyone but Niemöller was released that afternoon. Things had entered a new phase.

Niemöller was in jail for eight months, but on the day of his release the Gestapo promptly rearrested him. They were known for this unpleasant tactic. Hitler could not abide the freedom of someone so outspokenly against him, so he honored Pastor Niemöller with the distinction of being a "personal prisoner" of the Führer for the next seven years, which Niemöller spent in Dachau. He would be freed by the Allies in 1945.

Hildebrandt began preaching at Dahlem, his sermons no less fiery than Niemöller's. There were always Gestapo officers in the congregation. On July 18, in direct contravention of the new laws, Hildebrandt read aloud the list of those for whom intercessory prayers were being asked. He then took up an extra collection explicitly for the work of the Confessing Church. He instructed that the money be placed on the Lord's Table at the altar, where it was dedicated to God and God's work with a prayer. The Gestapo usually turned a blind eye to such breaches of the laws, but that day an officer brazenly went forward and took the money.

After this, Hildebrandt was arrested. A scene ensued in which Hildebrandt protested his arrest. Then the congregation joined in, growing louder and louder. The noisy crowd followed as the Gestapo officers escorted Hildebrandt outside to their car. The congregation crowded around the car, continuing their protest, and watched as the Gestapo officers tried to start the car and failed. After several embarrassing minutes, the humiliated Gestapo officers conceded defeat, got out of the car, and began walking with their prisoner toward headquarters. They were suddenly the objects of a jeering congregation, outraged that their pastor was being taken from them. Hildebrandt was taken to the Gestapo headquarters on the Alexanderplatz.

He then was taken to the Plötzensee prison. Bonhoeffer and his other friends feared for his life there. As a Jew, he was much more likely to be mistreated. Hans von Dohnanyi stepped into the fray and was able to get him out two days earlier than the prescribed twenty-eight. The early release enabled him to leave for Switzerland undetected by the authorities. Without this extraordinary intervention, he would have had to remain in the country and likely would have been rearrested as Niemöller had. As a non-Aryan, he probably would not have survived. From Switzerland, Hildebrandt went to London where he immediately became assistant pastor with his old friend Julius Rieger at St. George's. There he continued to work with refugees, and with Bishop Bell and his other ecumenical contacts. But Bonhoeffer would miss his friend.

In Berlin, the Confessing Church planned a service of intercession to be held at Niemöller's church in Dahlem on August 8. The church was cordoned off, but Niemöller's congregation, like its pastor, was made of sterner stuff than most, and things erupted into another demonstration against the Nazis. The crowds refused to disperse for hours. Two hundred and fifty of the faithful were arrested and taken to the Alexanderplatz.

The Collective Pastorates

Throughout the summer of 1937, Bonhoeffer oversaw the fifth six-month course at Finkenwalde. He was also completing work on his manuscript for a book on the Sermon on the Mount that had been taking form in his thoughts since about 1932. The book, to be called *Nachfolge* (*Discipleship*), appeared in November 1937. It would become one of the most influential Christian books of the twentieth century.

When the summer term was over, Bonhoeffer and Bethge took a holiday trip to the Königsee and to Grainau, near Ettal, in the Bavarian Alps. After this they went up to Göttingen to visit Sabine and Gerhard and their girls. It was in Göttingen that Bonhoeffer received a surprise telephone call from Stettin, informing him that the Gestapo had closed down Finkenwalde. The doors had been sealed. An era had ended.

Bonhoeffer tried everything to appeal the closing of Finkenwalde. But it was clear by the end of 1937 that Finkenwalde would not reopen. Still, Bonhoeffer knew this didn't have to mean the end of the illegal seminaries. They would continue in the form of a *Sammelvikariat* (collective pastorates).

The process began by finding a church whose senior pastor was sympathetic to the Confessing Church and placing a number of "apprentice vicars" with him. Theoretically, they would be assisting him, but would actually receive education in the Finkenwalde mode. The first, at Köslin, was about a hundred miles northeast of Stettin. The second was even more remote, about thirty miles farther east. In Schlawe, Bethge would be the director of studies. This group of ordinands lived east of Schlawe in what Bethge described as "the rambling, wind-battered parsonage in Gross-Schlönwitz, at the boundary of the church district." Bonhoeffer split his time between these idylls, traveling between Köslin and Schlawe on his motorcycle, weather permitting.

In 1939 the vicarage in Schlawe was no longer available, but even this was no hardship. The ordinands relocated to Sigurdshof, an even more remote location than Gross-Schlönwitz. It was as if a bird were leading them farther and farther away from the cares of the present and into a realm deep in the heart of a German fairy tale. Bethge wrote:

> The small house was two miles south of the village on the estate, and it was more secluded than anywhere they had lived up to that point. Four tiny windows looked out the front onto a little-used courtyard, under an overhanging roof and through luxurious climbing plants. In the back the idyllic Wipper River flowed by. . . . There was no electricity. . . . Anyone who did not find even this situation quiet enough could withdraw to a hunting lodge farther away in the forest. . . .
>
> We are anxious about our coal; and besides that, we have no paraffin, so we have to use candles. We all stay in one room, and someone plays [an instrument] or reads aloud.[12]

CHAPTER 8

THE GREAT DECISION

1938–1939

*I must live through this difficult period of our national history
with the Christian people of Germany. . . . Christians in
Germany will face the terrible alternative of either willing the
defeat of their nation in order that Christian civilization may
survive, or willing the victory of their nation and thereby
destroying our civilization. I know which of these alternatives
I must choose, but I cannot make that choice in security.*

—DIETRICH BONHOEFFER TO REINHOLD NIEBUHR, JULY 1939

The year 1938 was hugely tumultuous for Germany and the rest of Europe. It was certainly so for the Bonhoeffers, and for Dietrich it did not begin well at all. On January 11 he was arrested at a Confessing Church meeting in Dahlem. Gestapo officers appeared, arrested all thirty attendees, and interrogated them at the Alexanderplatz headquarters for seven hours before releasing them. Bonhoeffer learned he was henceforth banned from Berlin.

But knowing many people in high places, Bonhoeffer was almost never without recourse. Karl Bonhoeffer's eminence was somehow brought to bear on the situation, and he persuaded the Gestapo to make the ban exclusively related to work. So Dietrich could still travel to Berlin for personal and family matters.

Bonhoeffer had many reasons to believe that Hitler's luck would soon run out. Hitler's troubles had begun on November 5, 1937. He summoned his generals to a meeting in which he spelled out his plans for war. For four hours the megalomaniac scrawled a recipe of how he would soon have the world agog at his military genius: "I'll cook them a stew that they'll choke on!" He told the stunned generals that he would first attack Austria and Czechoslovakia to eliminate the possibility of trouble on Germany's eastern flank, and it was imperative that England be mollified for the moment since the English were a serious military threat.

The generals left this meeting in various states of shock and fury. What they had just heard was distilled madness. The foreign minister, Baron von Neurath, literally had several heart attacks. General Ludwig Beck found it all "shattering"; what he heard from Hitler that day would set him on his own mutinous course.

From that meeting forward, the generals were intent on removing him. Beck did all he could to influence them to stage a coup d'etat. Finally, to make as bold a public statement as possible, he resigned. This ought to have shaken the nation to its roots—and to have defenestrated the Nazis en masse. But by maintaining his dignified aristocratic bearing, Beck fluffed the full effect of his exit. He didn't want to draw too much attention to himself, for that would have been unseemly, so he departed with such nobility that hardly anyone heard him go.

Hitler further wiped the slate clean by announcing on the morning of February 4—Bonhoeffer's thirty-second birthday—a drastic reordering of the whole German military. It was a bold, sweeping decree: "From now on I take over personally the command of the whole armed forces." In a single stroke he abolished the War Ministry and created in its place the *Oberkommando der Wehrmacht* (OKW), making himself its head.

The Austrian *Anschluss*

Having successfully dealt with the military, Hitler could once again settle down and peacefully focus on how to take over Europe. Appropriately enough, his first toddling steps toward war and conquest were in the direction of his birthplace, Austria. In March 1938, he brought an entire nation into the Nazi fold with the annexation (*Anschluss*) of Austria. For many Germans, the *Anschluss* was a giddy moment. What had been taken from them through Versailles would now be returned to them—with interest—by their benevolent Führer.

In ecclesiastical circles, Bishop Sasse of Thuringia was first in line for sycophancy. His telegram to Hitler has been preserved: "My *Führer*, I report: in a great historic hour all the pastors of the Thuringian Evangelical Church, obeying an inner command, have with joyful hearts taken an oath of loyalty to *Führer* and Reich. . . . One God—one obedience in the faith. Hail, my *Führer!*"

The new head of the Reichskirche was Dr. Friedrich Werner. For his obsequious gesture, he chose the Führer's birthday. On April 20 he published in the *Legal Gazette* a sweeping ordinance demanding that every single pastor in Germany take an oath of obedience to Adolf Hitler.

Werner's decree brought bitter division to the Confessing Church at a time when things were already fragile. Many Confessing pastors were tired of fighting, and they thought that taking the oath was a mere formality, hardly worth losing one's career. Others took the oath, but with torn consciences, heartsick over what they were doing. But Bonhoeffer and others saw it as a cynical calculation and pushed the Confessing Church to stand against it. The church did not. Karl Barth wrote from Switzerland:

I am most deeply shocked by that decision and the arguments used to support it, after I have read and reread them. . . . Was this defeat possible, permissible or necessary? Was there and is there really no one among you at all who can lead you back to the simplicity of the straight and narrow way? . . . No one who beseeches you not to jeopardize the future credibility of the Confessing Church in this dreadful way?[1]

On May 28, Hitler informed his military commanders of his plans to march into Czechoslovakia and end its cartographical existence. Compulsory civilian service was enacted in June, and throughout the summer, Germany leaned toward war.

Fleeing Germany

The Leibholzes began to wonder whether their days in Germany would soon be over. A law was about to take effect requiring every Jewish person's passport to be emended if the person's given name was not obviously Jewish: Israel had to be added as a middle name for men, and Sarah for women. Hans von Dohnanyi urged the Leibholzes to leave while they could. If war broke out, Germany's borders would be sealed. Sabine and Gert heard stories of Jews being abducted at night and humiliated. Every time the doorbell rang they were frightened, not knowing what trouble lay behind it. They had traveled to Switzerland or Italy on vacations and felt the freedom of being outside Germany. "Each time that we journeyed back to Göttingen," Sabine recalled, "something like an iron band seemed to tighten round my heart with every kilometre that brought us nearer to the town."

Finally they made preparations to leave. It was a monumental and heart-wrenching decision. Sabine and Gert first went to Berlin where they discussed all the final details with the family, who had already begun to use code words in phone and written communications.

They still hoped that with the imminent coup of which Dohnanyi was informing them, they would be able to return before very long. Perhaps they would only be away a few weeks.

When they returned to Göttingen on September 8, Bethge and Bonhoeffer followed from Berlin in Bonhoeffer's car. The plan was to accompany them for part of the journey to the Swiss border the following day. Everything was conducted in utter secrecy. Even the girls' nanny could not know.

The next day was a Friday. The nanny woke the girls at six thirty and began to get them ready for school. Suddenly their mother came into the room and announced that they were not going to school. They would be going on a trip to Wiesbaden! Eleven-year-old Marianne suspected something was afoot. They never went to Wiesbaden. But she was wise enough to know that if they were about to leave their home, she mustn't let on. Sabine told the girls' nanny they would be back on Monday.

The Leibholzes' car was packed full, but not too full. They drove away in the two cars. When they felt it was safe, Sabine told the girls that they weren't going to Wiesbaden after all. They were going to cross the Swiss border. "They may close the frontier because of the crisis," she said.

Many years later Marianne recalled that day:

> The roof of our car was open, the sky was deep blue, the coun-
> tryside looked marvelous in the hot sunshine. I felt there was
> complete solidarity between the four grown-ups. I knew that
> unaccustomed things would be asked of us children from now
> on but felt proud of now being allowed to share the real troubles
> of the adults. I thought if I could do nothing against the Nazis
> myself I must at the very least co-operate with the grown-ups
> who could. Christiane and I spent most the time singing in the
> car, folk songs and rather militant songs about freedom, my
> mother, Uncle Dietrich and "Uncle" Bethge singing with us.[2]

After seeing Sabine, Gert, and the girls off, Bonhoeffer and Bethge returned to Göttingen, where they stayed in the Leibholzes' house for several weeks. There Bonhoeffer wrote his small devotional classic, *Life Together.** While Bonhoeffer wrote, the Czechoslovakian crisis was front and center. Hitler publicly maintained that the German-speaking populations of Europe belonged to Germany. The Austrian *Anschluss* had been portrayed not as an act of aggression, but as a benevolent father welcoming his children home. The Sudetenland situation was portrayed in the same way.

The army generals were aching for Hitler to march on Czechoslovakia, not because they thought it wise, but because they thought it so patently foolish that it would give them the opportunity they had been waiting for. They would seize Hitler and take over the government.

As things stood that September, Hitler was on the verge of marching into Czechoslovakia, and all the European leaders were expecting him to do so. It seemed inevitable. They were preparing to stop him by military means, and would have succeeded; Germany was simply not ready to wage war on the scale that would have been necessary. The scene was set. But what played out on the world stage in the weeks ahead was stranger than fiction.

The breathtaking climax of this magnificent drama was destroyed by Britain's prime minister, Neville Chamberlain, who suddenly appeared in the unprecedented role of appeaser *ex machina*. The sixty-nine-year-old prime minister had never been in an airplane before, but he would now fly seven hours from London to Berchtesgaden on the far side of Germany to meet with the ill-mannered tyrant.

His badly timed efforts would serve for generations as the

---

* He had already dictated parts of it at Gross-Schlönwitz. Hans-Werner Jensen, an ordinand, recalled typing it to Bonhoeffer's dictation.

textbook example of cheap grace in geopolitical terms: it was "peace" on the house, with a side order of Czechoslovakia. In a year, when he surged across Poland, Hitler would laugh at Chamberlain. When the Nazis demanded that every Jew in Germany have a J stamped on his or her passport, it was clear the Leibholzes could not return. They would leave Switzerland for London. There Bonhoeffer connected them with Bishop Bell and Julius Rieger, who welcomed them as they had welcomed so many Jewish refugees from the Third Reich. Franz Hildebrandt, whom they knew very well, was also on hand to help them get established. Gerhard eventually was able to get a lectureship at Magdalen College, Oxford, where C. S. Lewis was at the time.

Kristallnacht

The infamous events of early November 1938 began on the seventh when a seventeen-year-old German Jew shot and killed an official in the German Embassy in Paris. As with the burning of the Reichstag, the shooting was just the pretext Hitler and the Nazi leaders needed. In a "spontaneous" series of demonstrations, evils would be unleashed against the Jews of Germany on a terrible scale.

Hitler gave the command to take action against the Jews, but to execute this action, he looked to the services of Reinhard Heydrich, Himmler's second in command at the SS. At 1:20 a.m., the night following the Paris assassination, he sent an urgent Teletype message to every Gestapo station across Germany. The orders gave explicit directions on how to perpetrate the events of what has come to be known as the *Kristallnacht* (Night of Broken Glass). Homes and businesses were destroyed and looted, synagogues were set aflame, and Jews were beaten and killed.

In his Bible that day or the next, Bonhoeffer was reading Psalm 74. This was the text he happened to be meditating upon. What he read startled him, and with his pencil he put a vertical line in the margin to mark it, with an exclamation point next to the line. He also underlined the second half of verse 8: *"Sie verbrennen alle Häuser Gottes im Lande."* ("They burn all God's houses in the land.") Next to the verse he wrote: "9.11.38." This was when Bonhoeffer most clearly saw the connection: to lift one's hand against the Jews was to lift one's hand against God himself. The Nazis were attacking God by attacking his people.

Hans-Werner Jensen recalled that Bonhoeffer's awareness of what the Jews were going through immediately following *Kristallnacht* caused him to be "driven by a great inner restlessness, a holy anger. . . . During those ugly days we learned to understand— not just human revenge, but the prayer of the so-called psalms of vengeance which give over to God alone the case of the inno- cent, 'for his name's sake.' It was not apathy and passiveness which Dietrich Bonhoefer derived from them, but for him prayer was the display of the strongest possible activity."

It's impossible to say when Bonhoeffer joined the conspiracy, mainly because he was always in the midst of it, even before it could have been called a conspiracy. The Bonhoeffer family had relation- ships with many powerful people in the government, most of whom shared their anti-Hitler views.

Then there was Hans von Dohnanyi, Bonhoeffer's brother-in- law, who was one of the conspiracy's leaders. In 1933, he was assigned to the *Reichsjustizminister*, Franz Gürtner, and for the first time he had a blood-spattered front-row seat at the inner workings of the Nazi leadership. But he deftly avoided any connection to the party, which caused him serious trouble now and again.

During 1938, Dohnanyi helped Ewald von Kleist-Schmenzin provide British intelligence with information about Hitler and the Nazis, trying to influence them into taking a tough stand against Hitler before he marched into Austria and the Sudetenland.

The head of the Abwehr (German Military Intelligence) was Wilhelm Canaris. Knowing Dohnanyi's position on Hitler, Canaris appointed Dohnanyi to his staff and asked him to compile a file of the Nazis' atrocities. A year later, when the war against Poland was launched, Dohnanyi documented the barbarity of the SS *Einsatzgruppen*, even though many of the top generals themselves knew nothing about it. Canaris knew that the evidence of these atrocities would be crucial in convincing those generals and others to join the coup when the time came.

Much of this information collected by Dohnanyi found its way to his brothers-in-law and their families. Before others in Germany knew of them, the Bonhoeffers heard of the mass murders in Poland, the systematic burning of synagogues there, and much else. Things that no one would know about for years were known in the Bonhoeffer household almost as quickly as they happened. Dohnanyi kept a file of these things. It was labeled "the Chronicle of Shame," but it later became known as the Zossen File, because it was eventually hidden—and found—in Zossen.

Back to America

On January 23, Bonhoeffer's mother informed him that she had seen a notice ordering all men born in 1906 and 1907 to register with the military. Bonhoeffer's hand would now be forced. There was one possible solution. Bonhoeffer might be able to have his military call-up deferred for a year. Perhaps in the meantime he might return to America and work in the ecumenical movement. As he thought about the possibilities, he decided he must speak with Reinhold Niebuhr, who had been his professor at Union. Niebuhr was giving the prestigious Gifford Lectures in Edinburgh that year and would soon be in Sussex, England. Bonhoeffer wanted to visit Sabine and Gert, for whom living abroad had not been easy. And he wanted very much to see Bishop Bell. It was decided: he would go to England.

On March 10, Bonhoeffer and Bethge took a night train to

Ostend on the Belgian coast. The next day they made the Channel crossing. On March 15, Hitler breached Chamberlain's Munich agreement by devouring more of Czechoslovakia. To save face, the British prime minister vowed to declare war if Hitler marched on Poland. War was coming.

In England, Bonhoeffer was thrilled to see Franz Hildebrandt again and Julius Rieger. On March 29 he traveled with the Leibholzes to Oxford, and on April 3, with Julius Rieger and Gerhard Leibholz, he went to Sussex to see Niebuhr, hoping for assistance. Bonhoeffer explained that getting a solid and official invitation to teach at Union for a year would solve his dilemma, but it would be needed quickly. Niebuhr leaped into action.

The next day, the Reichskirche published the Godesberg Declaration, signed by Dr. Werner. It declared that National Socialism was a natural continuation of "the work of Martin Luther" and stated that the "Christian faith is the unbridgeable religious opposite to Judaism." It also said: "Supra-national and international church structure of a Roman Catholic or world-Protestant character is a political degeneration of Christianity."

The Provisional Committee of the World Council of Churches wrote a manifesto in response, drafted by Karl Barth. It repudiated the idea that race, national identity, or ethnic background had anything to do with actual Christian faith and declared, "The Gospel of Jesus Christ is the fulfillment of the Jewish hope. . . . The Christian church . . . rejoices in the maintenance of community with those of the Jewish race who have accepted the Gospel."

Bonhoeffer knew that he might be called up any day, but all he could do was wait and pray. Meanwhile, Niebuhr set a number of things in motion. On May 11, Henry Leiper sent Bonhoeffer a formal letter offering a joint position with Union and with Leiper's organization, the Central Bureau of Interchurch Aid. For Leiper, Bonhoeffer would serve as pastor to German refugees in New York. He would also lecture in the theological summer school of Union and Columbia, and in the fall he would lecture during Union's regular term. The grand position that Leiper had created just for him should occupy Bonhoeffer for "at least the next two or three years." Meanwhile, Paul Lehmann, thrilled at the prospect of having his old friend back, fired off urgent letters to more than thirty colleges—no mean feat in the days before computers—asking whether they would be interested in Bonhoeffer lecturing.

On May 22, Bonhoeffer received a notice to report for military duty. He contacted the necessary authorities, informing them of the official invitations from Union and Leiper. On June 4 he was on his way to America.

On June 12, 1939, a week shy of eight years since leaving New York, Bonhoeffer entered the great harbor of America for the second time. But things were quite different now, for him and for the city. The Manhattan skyline did not seem to grin at him as it did before, nor had it sprouted a single new tooth since his departure. The building frenzy and the vibrancy and the ferment of the Jazz Age were gone. The Great Depression that had then taken its first steps was now ten years old.

He had not been in New York twenty-four hours, but Bonhoeffer was already deeply out of sorts. His mind continued to churn about the situation back home, wondering how long he should stay in America, and whether he ought to have come at all. But ever the master of his emotions, he didn't betray any of this inner turmoil to his hosts. His diary gives us his thoughts:

13th June, 1939— . . . Very friendly and "informal" reception. All that's missing is Germany, the brethren. The first lonely hours are hard. I do not understand why I am here, whether it was a sensible thing to do, whether the results will be worthwhile. In the evening, last of all, the readings and thoughts about work at home. I have now been almost two weeks without knowing what is going on there. It is hard to bear.

14th June, 1939—Breakfast on the verandah at eight. It poured
during the night. Everything is fresh and clean. Then prayers.
I was almost overcome by the short prayer—the whole family
knelt down—in which we thought of the German brethren.
Then reading, writing, going out to issue invitations for the
evening. In the evening about twenty-five people, pastors,
teachers, with wives and friends. Very friendly conversations
without getting anywhere.

15th June, 1939—Since yesterday evening I haven't been able
to stop thinking of Germany. I would not have thought it
possible that at my age, after so many years abroad, one could
get so dreadfully homesick. What was in itself a wonderful
motor expedition this morning to a female acquaintance in the
country, i.e., in the hills, became almost unbearable. We sat for
an hour and chattered, not in a silly way, true, but about things
which left me completely cold—whether it is possible to get
a good musical education in New York, about the education
of children, etc., etc., and I thought how usefully I could be
spending these hours in Germany. I would gladly have taken
the next ship home.[3]

Torn between his hatred of wasted words and his deep respect for
mannerly behavior, Bonhoeffer was the very definition of unsettled.
Alone in his room, he wrote Leiper, saying that he must go back
"within a year at the latest" and explaining himself, obviously feeling
guilty for having led anyone astray in expectations. But then at long
last he found peace in the Scriptures, into which he now settled himself: "How glad I was to begin the readings again in the evening and
find 'My heart shall rejoice in thy salvation' (Ps. 13.5)."

The next morning he visited the World's Fair in Queens. He
spent the afternoon there, amidst the crowds. When he returned
to his room that evening, he was delighted to have solitude again,

to think and pray. He spent most of the following Saturday in the Union library, working. He studied issues of the *Christian Century* for an essay he was writing. But all the while he was pining for a letter from Germany, telling him of the situation there. Nothing in his life could quite compare with what he felt. He was more unsettled, more profoundly out of sorts, than ever. He seemed cut off from a part of himself, divided from himself by an ocean, wandering the streets of New York like a ghost:

> It is almost unbearable. . . . Today God's Word says, "I am coming soon" (Rev. 3.11). There is no time to lose, and here I am wasting days, perhaps weeks. In any case, it seems like that at the moment. Then I say to myself again, "It is cowardice and weakness to run away here now." Will I ever be able to do any really significant work here? Disquieting political news from Japan. If it becomes unsettled now I am definitely going back to Germany. I cannot stay outside [Germany] by myself. That is quite clear. My whole life is still over there.[4]

On the morning of June 20, he finally got a letter from his parents. But still nothing from the brethren. That day he was to have an important lunch meeting with Henry Leiper. They met at the National Arts Club on Gramercy Park. Afterward he wrote in his diary: "The decision has been made. I have refused. They were clearly disappointed, and rather upset. It probably means more for me than I can see at the moment. God alone knows what."

Years later, Leiper recalled their lunch meeting there, under the famous tiled ceiling of the exclusive club. He had obviously looked forward to the lunch as much as Bonhoeffer had dreaded it; he expected to discuss the nature of the work they would do together. "What was my surprise and dismay," Leiper said, "to learn from my guest that he had just received an urgent appeal from his colleagues in Germany to return at once for important tasks which they felt he alone could perform." We do not know to what Bonhoeffer was referring. It's possible his parents' letter included a coded reference to the conspiracy, something that seemed urgent to him and that had decided his course. In any case, he was determined to obey God and was sure he was doing so in deciding to return to Germany.

That evening in his diary Bonhoeffer ruminated about the decision, puzzled by the strange mystery of it all:

> It is remarkable how I am never quite clear about the motives for any of my decisions. Is that a sign of confusion, of inner dishonesty, or is it a sign that we are guided without our knowing, or is it both? . . . Today the reading speaks dreadfully harshly of God's incorruptible judgement. He certainly sees how much personal feeling, how much anxiety there is in today's decision, however brave it may seem. The reasons one gives for an action to others and to one's self are certainly inadequate. One can give a reason for everything. In the last resort one acts from a level which remains hidden from us. So one can only ask God to judge us and to forgive us. . . . At the end of the day I can only ask God to give a merciful judgement on today and all its decisions. It is now in his hand.[5]

He set his face toward Berlin. Somehow he was again at peace. He had been in New York twenty-six days.

> 7th July, 1939—Farewell half past eleven, sail at half past twelve. Manhattan by night; the moon over the skyscrapers. It is very hot. The visit is at an end. I am glad to have been over and glad that I am on the way home. Perhaps I have learnt more in this month than in a whole year nine years ago; at least I have acquired some important insight for all future decisions. Probably this visit will have a great effect on me. *In the middle of the Atlantic Ocean* . . .[6]

July 1939. Dietrich with his twin sister, Sabine, in London, just after his return from America and before his final return to Germany.
(Art Resource, NY)

He was in England for ten days. He did not visit Bishop Bell, but he saw Franz Hildebrandt and Julius Rieger again, and he spent time with his beloved Sabine, Gerhard, and the girls.

He arrived in Berlin on July 27 and immediately traveled to Sigurdshof to continue his work. Unbeknownst to him, Hellmut Traub had ably taken over where Bonhoeffer had left off. Traub recalled his surprise at seeing Bonhoeffer suddenly returned to them:

> I was happy to know that Bonhoeffer was not in Germany, but safe from the coming reign of terror, and the catastrophe which I was convinced would follow. He must not perish in it. He knew about the resurgence of the Church, about the inner necessity (and not just the external necessity conditioned by

the German Christians) of the Confessing Church whose
destiny he had helped to shape; the best of liberal theology
from Harnack's time, as well as the most recent movement
of dialectical theology, were alive in him, and equally so
an amazingly extensive general, philosophical, literary and
artistic education. His openness and his free and unpreju-
diced conviction that the Church must undergo a change,
renew itself, justified the confidence he enjoyed in foreign
churches. . . . He was practically predestined to rebuild the
Protestant church after the débâcle which most certainly was
in store for us. . . . Over and above this, and apart from the
great danger of his situation, Bonhoeffer was sure to find no
mercy, as he was bound to be a conscientious objector. There
was no room for him in this present-day Germany, because
we believed that *then*, later, we would be in real, deepest need
of him; *then* his time would come.

And then one day, after a short message that he was
returning, Bonhoeffer stood before us. This was quite un-
expected—indeed, there was always something extraordinary
about him, even when the circumstances were quite ordinary.
I was immediately up in arms, blurting out how could he
come back after it had cost so much trouble to get him into
safety—safety for us, for our cause; here everything was lost
anyway. He very calmly lit a cigarette. Then he said that he
had made a mistake in going to America. He did not himself
understand now why he had done it. . . . It is this fact—that
he abandoned in all clarity many great possibilities for his
own development in the free countries, that he returned to
dismal slavery and a dark future, but also to his own reality—which gave to everything he told us then a strong and
joyful firmness, such as only arises out of realized freedom.
He knew he had taken a clear step, though the actualities
before him were still quite unclear.[7]

Life at the two collective pastorates in eastern Pomerania continued that August. But the sense of war was imminent, and they were so close to Poland, where it would surely begin, that Bonhoeffer thought it too dangerous to remain there. He decided they must leave. So the Köslin and Sigurdshof terms were prematurely ended, and on August 26, Bonhoeffer was back in Berlin.

The End of Germany

Neville Chamberlain had vowed that Britain would defend Poland if Hitler attacked it. That time had come. But Hitler couldn't simply attack. He had to make it look like self-defense. So on August 22, he told his generals, "I shall give a propagandist reason for starting the war; never mind whether it is plausible or not. The victor will not be asked afterward whether he told the truth."

The plan was for the SS, dressed in Polish uniforms, to attack a German radio station on the Polish border. To make the whole thing authentic, they would need German "casualties." They decided to use concentration camp inmates, whom they vilely referred to as *Konserven* (canned goods). These victims of Germany would be dressed as German soldiers. In the end only one man was murdered for this purpose, via lethal injection, and afterward shot several times to give the appearance that he had been killed by Polish soldiers. The deliberate murder of a human being for the purposes of deceiving the world seems a perfectly fitting inaugural act for what was to follow. This took place on schedule, August 31.

In "retaliation," German troops marched into Poland at dawn on September 1. Göring's Luftwaffe rained hell from the skies, deliberately killing civilians. Civilians were murdered more carefully on the ground. It was a coldly deliberate act of terror by intentional mass murder, never before seen in modern times, and it was the Poles' first bitter taste of the Nazi ruthlessness they would come to know so well.

Hitler gave a speech to the Reichstag, casting himself in the role of aggrieved victim. "You know the endless attempts I made for a peaceful clarification and understanding of the problem of Austria," he said, "and later of the problem of the Sudetenland, Bohemia and Moravia. It was all in vain. . . . I am wrongly judged if my love of peace and patience are mistaken for weakness or even cowardice. . . . I have therefore resolved to speak to Poland in the same language that Poland for months past has used toward us."

Admiral Canaris, the head of the Abwehr, had long dreaded this hour. He was overcome with emotion at the implications of it all. Hans Bernd Gisevius, a diplomat whom Canaris had recruited to work with him in the Resistance, was at OKW headquarters that day. They ran into each other in a back stairway, and Canaris drew Gisevius aside. "This means the end of Germany," he said.

It now only remained for Britain to declare war. For two days the British engaged in diplomatic back and forth, but at some point someone lent Chamberlain a vertebra, and on Sunday Great Britain declared war.

That morning Dietrich and Karl-Friedrich were a few minutes from home, discussing the events of the last days. It was a warm, humid morning, with low-hanging cloud cover over the city. Suddenly there were sirens. World War II had begun. By war's end more than 80 of the 150 young men from Finkenwalde and the collective pastorates would be killed.

The war put Bonhoeffer in a strange position. He knew he could not fight for Hitler's Germany, but he was extraordinarily supportive when it came to the young men who did not see things his way. He also knew he had options they did not. Albrecht Schönherr remembered the climate:

Through the Nazi propaganda and this whole blurring of the situation, we had the feeling, well, in the end we really must step in; the Fatherland must be defended. Not with a very

good conscience, of course not. Above all not with enthusiasm. . . . After all, it was very clearly the case that whoever
refused the draft in the case of war would be beheaded, would
be executed. . . . Bonhoeffer did not say, you may not go. . . . I
know that Bonhoeffer himself was sad that he had supported a
man who completely refused the draft and then was executed.
It was a very strange situation in which we all stood.[8]

When the fighting in Poland ended, it seemed safe to resume
the collective pastorates, at least the one in Sigurdshof. Eight ordinands arrived there, and Bonhoeffer picked up where he had left
off. He alternated between the otherworldly, fairyland idyll of the
Pomeranian woods and the churning intrigue of *über*-present Berlin.

In Berlin he met with Dohnanyi, who told him everything, as
he always had. But Bonhoeffer now heard things he had not heard
before, things that would fundamentally alter his thinking.

Dohnanyi told him that now, under the dark cover of war,
Hitler had unleashed horrors that beggared description, that made
the usual horrors of war quaint things of the past. Reports from
Poland indicated that the SS were committing unspeakable atrocities, things unheard of in civilized times. Dohnanyi's primary source
was his boss, Admiral Canaris.

Canaris and the others in the German military leadership
thought that Hitler's bestial nature was unfortunate, but they had
no idea it was something that he cultivated and celebrated, that it
was part of an ideology that had been waiting for this opportunity
to leap at the throats of every Jew and Pole, priest and aristocrat,
and tear them to pieces. Since the SS perpetrated the most wicked
acts, Hitler could keep the worst of it from his military leaders. But
reports leaked out. Many generals were beside themselves.

General Blaskowitz sent Hitler a memo describing the horrors
he had seen. He was profoundly concerned about the effect on the
German soldiers. If hardened military leaders were disturbed, one

can imagine the effect these things would have on the young men who had never seen a battlefield. General Bock read Blaskowitz's memo and found its descriptions "hair-raising."

Just as Hitler had been planning for years to enslave the Poles and kill the Jews, he had been planning to murder every German with a disability. Preparations for the T-4 euthanasia program had been under way for years. Now they hit the ground running. In August 1939 every doctor and midwife in the country was notified that they must register all children born with genetic defects—*retroactive to 1936*. In September, when the war began, so, too, began the killing of these "defectives." In the next few years five thousand small children were killed. It wasn't until later that fall that attention was formally focused on the other "incurables."

On September 27, the day of Warsaw's surrender, Hitler convened his generals and announced plans to make war on the western frontier too. He would attack Belgium and Holland. And then France and England. And Denmark and Norway. Again, the generals were thunderstruck by what they heard.

Beck told Dohnanyi to update his Chronicle of Shame. To that end, Dohnanyi obtained actual film footage of many SS atrocities in Poland. To avoid another *Dolchstoss* (stab-in-the-back) legend from arising when Hitler was killed and Germany "defeated" by the Allies, it was vital to have proof of the Nazi atrocities.

It was worse than anything Bonhoeffer had dreamed. But he couldn't even share what he knew with his best friends. It had become too dangerous. More than ever now, he was alone with God, and he looked to God's judgment upon his actions. This was when he began to realize that he was already part of the conspiracy to remove Hitler.

CHAPTER 9

FROM CONFESSION TO CONSPIRACY

1940–1942

The German people will be burdened with a guilt the world will not forget in a hundred years.

—HENNING VON TRESCKOW

We now realized that mere confession, no matter how courageous, inescapably meant complicity with the murderers.

—EBERHARD BETHGE

There were more conversations and meetings, and Bonhoeffer was at the center of many of them. He was in the heart of the conspiracy, lending emotional support and encouragement to those more directly involved, such as his brother Klaus and his brother-in-law Dohnanyi. He didn't have qualms about it, but as a leader in the Confessing Church,

Bonhoeffer's situation was a complicated one. He wasn't free to do as he pleased.

Meanwhile, the conspiracy moved ahead with renewed vigor. Dohnanyi got in touch with Dr. Joseph Müller, a Munich lawyer with strong ties to the Vatican. Müller's assignment in October 1939 was to travel to Rome, seemingly on official Abwehr business. He convinced the pope to agree to act as an intermediary between Britain and the fledgling German government that would form following Hitler's demise. It was all very promising. The conspirators planned to launch the coup when Hitler gave the green light to attack the West.

No one has better attempted to explain the seeming paradox of a Christian involved in a plot to assassinate a head of state than Eberhard Bethge:

> Bonhoeffer introduced us in 1935 to the problem of what we today call political resistance. The levels of confession and of resistance could no longer be kept neatly apart. The escalating persecution of the Jews generated an increasingly intolerable situation, especially for Bonhoeffer himself. We now realized that mere confession, no matter how courageous, inescapably meant complicity with the murderers, even though there would always be new acts of refusing to be co-opted and even though we would preach "Christ alone" Sunday after Sunday. During the whole time the Nazi state never considered it necessary to prohibit such preaching. Why should it?
>
> Thus we were approaching the borderline between confession and resistance; and if we did not cross this border, our confession was going to be no better than cooperation with the criminals. And so it became clear where the problem lay for the Confessing Church: we were resisting by way of confession, but we were not confessing by way of resistance.[1]

Bonhoeffer would get his hands dirty, not because he had grown impatient, but because God was speaking to him about further steps of obedience.

Crossing the Rubicon

After months of postponement, Hitler ordered his armies to march west in May of 1940. On the tenth, German units attacked Holland. The Dutch succumbed in five days. Belgium was next, and soon German tanks roared across France. On June 14, German troops marched into Paris, and three days later *le mot oncle* was heard round the world.

Meanwhile, on the far side of the continent, Bonhoeffer and Bethge were visiting the pastorate of one of the Finkenwalde brothers in eastern Prussia. After a pastors' meeting that morning, they took a ferry across to the peninsula and found an outdoor café in the sun. Suddenly a trumpet fanfare on the radio loudspeakers announced a special news flash: *France has surrendered!*

People went wild. Some of them leaped up and stood on chairs; others stood on tables. Everyone threw out his arm in the Nazi salute and burst into "Deutschland über Alles" and then the "Horst Wessel Song." It was a pandemonium of patriotism, and Bonhoeffer and Bethge were pinned like beetles. Bonhoeffer stood up and threw out his arm in the "Heil, Hitler!" salute. As Bethge stood there gawking, Bonhoeffer whispered to him: "Are you crazy? Raise your arm! We'll have to run risks for many different things, but this silly salute is not one of them!"

It was then, Bethge realized, that Bonhoeffer had crossed a line. He was behaving conspiratorially. He didn't want to be thought of as an objector. He wanted to blend in. He didn't want to make an anti-Hitler statement; he had bigger fish to fry. Bethge said that he knew at that café in Memel, when Bonhoeffer was saluting Hitler, that his friend had crossed from "confession" to "resistance."

As his role in the conspiracy developed, Bonhoeffer continued his pastoral work and his writings. The last book he published in his lifetime was *Das Gebetbook der Bibel* (*The Prayerbook of the Bible*), which appeared in 1940. That a book on the Old Testament Psalms was published then is a testimony to Bonhoeffer's devotion to scholarly truth and his willingness to deceive the leaders of the Third Reich.

Bonhoeffer scholar Geffrey Kelly wrote, "One should make no mistake about it; in the context of Nazi Germany's bitter opposition to any manner of honoring of the Old Testament, this book, at the time of its publication, constituted an explosive declaration both politically and theologically." The book was a passionate declaration of the importance of the Old Testament to Christianity and to the church, and it was a bold and scholarly rebuke to Nazi efforts to undermine anything of Jewish origin.

In the book, Bonhoeffer linked the idea of Barthian grace with prayer by saying that we cannot reach God with our own prayers, but by praying "his" prayers—the Psalms of the Old Testament, which Jesus prayed—we effectively piggyback on them all the way to heaven.

The idea would have seemed impossibly "Jewish" for the Nazis, and it was too "Catholic" for many Protestants, who saw in recited prayers the "vain repetition" of the heathen. But, in one slim book, Bonhoeffer was nonetheless claiming that Jesus had given his imprimatur to the Psalms and to the Old Testament; that Christianity was unavoidably Jewish; that the Old Testament is not superseded by the New Testament, but is inextricably linked with it; and that Jesus was unavoidably Jewish.

Abwehr Agent Bonhoeffer

On July 14, 1940, Bonhoeffer was preaching at a church conference in Königsberg when the Gestapo arrived and broke up the meeting. They cited a new order forbidding such meetings, and the conference ended. No one was arrested, but Bonhoeffer saw that his ability to continue such pastoral work was coming to an end. Soon after, Bonhoeffer returned to Berlin and spoke with Dohnanyi about his plans going forward.

There was a great rivalry between the Abwehr and the Gestapo. But since they occupied separate spheres—just as the CIA and the FBI do in the United States—Dohnanyi reasoned that if the Abwehr officially employed Bonhoeffer, the Gestapo would be forced to leave him alone. It made sense for many reasons. Bonhoeffer would have great freedom of movement to continue his work as a pastor, and he would have the cover needed to expand his activities for the conspiracy. Another benefit was that as an invaluable member of Germany's Military Intelligence, Bonhoeffer was unlikely to be called into military service.

Dohnanyi's boss, General Oster, had said that National Socialism was "an ideology of such sinister immorality that traditional values and loyalties no longer applied." But for many in the Confessing Church, such deception was no different from lying. Bonhoeffer had moved into a very lonely place indeed.

Dohnanyi, Bethge, Bonhoeffer, Gisevius, and Oster discussed this arrangement in a meeting at the Bonhoeffer home that August. They decided to move forward. The day had come. Bonhoeffer had officially joined the conspiracy. He would be enfolded into the Abwehr's protection and, in the guise of a member of Military Intelligence, would be protected by Oster and Canaris.

The levels of deception were several. On the one hand, Bonhoeffer would be actually performing pastoral work and continuing his theological writing, as he wished to do. Officially this work was a front for his work as a Nazi agent in Military Intelligence. But unofficially his work in Military Intelligence was a front for his real work as a conspirator against the Nazi regime. In Luther's famous phrase, Bonhoeffer was indeed "sinning boldly."

That September, however, the RSHA (*Reichssicherheitshauptamt*), which also had a bitter rivalry with the Abwehr, caused Bonhoeffer further trouble. The RSHA was led by the waxy lamprey Reinhard Heydrich, who worked directly under Himmler. The RSHA now informed Bonhoeffer that because of what they termed "subversive activities," he was no longer allowed to speak in public. As a result, his role with the Abwehr would get more serious, and the cat-and-mouse game with Hitler's henchmen would begin in earnest. First of all, Dohnanyi wanted to get him away from the RSHA's interference. It was contrived to assign him Abwehr duties that took him to Munich.

In Munich, Bonhoeffer reconnected with Joseph Müller, the papal envoy for the Resistance. Bonhoeffer's work with the Resistance in Munich was now through him. Müller wangled an invitation for Bonhoeffer to live at Ettal, a picturesque Benedictine monastery nestled in the Garmisch-Partenkirchen region of the Bavarian Alps. For Bonhoeffer, it was a small dream come true. Here, in this Catholic bastion of resistance against the Nazis, he found profound peace and quiet, far from the mental noise of Berlin. Bonhoeffer became friendly with the prior and abbot, who invited him to stay as their guest as long as he liked, and beginning in November, he lived there through the winter.

Bonhoeffer's ministry to the brethren continued through packages and frequent letters. That year's Christmas letter was another beautiful "sermon meditation," this time on Isaiah 9:6–7 ("For unto us a child is born . . ."). He ruminated on the idea that things had changed forever, that they could never go back to the way they were before the war. But he explained that the idea one could ever go back to a time before troubles and death was false to begin with. The war was only showing them a deeper reality that always existed:

> Just as time-lapse photography makes visible, in an ever more compressed and penetrating form, movements that would otherwise not be thus grasped by our vision, so the war makes manifest in particularly drastic and unshrouded form that

which for years has become ever more dreadfully clear to us as the essence of the "world."[2]

At Ettal, Bonhoeffer often met with members of the conspiracy, such as Justice Minister Gürtner and Carl Goerdeler, the former mayor of Leipzig. Müller sometimes stopped by daily. On February 24, the Abwehr sent Bonhoeffer to Geneva. His main purpose was to make contact with Protestant leaders outside Germany, let them know about the conspiracy, and put out feelers about peace terms with the government that would take over. Müller was still having similar conversations at the Vatican with Catholic leaders.

But at first, Bonhoeffer couldn't even get into Switzerland. The Swiss border police insisted that someone inside Switzerland vouch for him as his guarantor. Bonhoeffer named Karl Barth, who was called, and assented, but not without some misgivings.

Like others at the time, Barth was perplexed about Bonhoeffer's mission. How could a Confessing Church pastor come to Switzerland in the midst of war? It seemed to him that Bonhoeffer must have somehow made peace with the Nazis. This was one of the casualties of the war, that trust itself seemed to die a thousand deaths.

Such doubts and questions from others would plague Bonhoeffer, but he certainly wasn't free to explain what he was doing to those outside his inner circle. People wondered how he escaped the fate of the rest of his generation. He was writing and traveling, meeting with this one and that one, going to movies and restaurants, and living a life of relative privilege and freedom while others were suffering and dying and being put in excruciating positions of moral compromise.

For those who knew that Bonhoeffer was working for the Abwehr, it was all the worse. Had he finally capitulated, this high-minded patrician moralist, who always was so unyielding and who demanded that others must be similarly unyielding? Was he the one who had said that "only those who cry out for the Jews may sing Gregorian chants" and who had put himself in the place of God by outrageously declaring that there was no salvation outside the Confessing Church?

Even if Bonhoeffer could have explained that he was in fact working against Hitler, many in the Confessing Church would still have been confused, and others would have been outraged. For a pastor to be involved in a plot whose linchpin was the assassination of the head of state during a time of war, when brothers and sons and fathers were giving their lives for their country, was unthinkable.

Bonhoeffer was in Switzerland a month. When he returned to Munich at the end of March, he discovered a letter from the Reich Writers' Guild informing him that he was henceforth prohibited from writing: no ruse would be sufficient to offset the offensively pro-Jewish content of his book on the Psalms.

The Commissar Order

April saw Nazi victories so stunning and rapid that most generals had lost all confidence in their ability to oppose Hitler. Yugoslavia, Greece, and Albania had been conquered, and General Rommel had triumphed in North Africa. Hitler seemed unstoppable, so most generals floated along with the rising German tide and could not be persuaded to lift a finger against him.

But Dohnanyi and Oster knew that persuading the top generals was the only hope of toppling Hitler. It had been earlier hoped that a grassroots movement could bring the Nazis down from below. But once Martin Niemöller was imprisoned, this possibility had evaporated. Beck, Dohnanyi, Oster, Canaris, Goerdeler, and the other conspirators did what they could during this year of Hitler's successes, but essentially they were stuck.

Then came June 6, 1941, and the notorious Commissar Order. The Commissar Order instructed the army to shoot and kill all captured Soviet military leaders. Hitler had allowed the army to avoid the most gruesome horrors in Poland. He knew they didn't have the stomach for it, and the soulless SS *Einsatzgruppen* had done the foulest and most inhuman deeds. But now he ordered the army itself to carry out the butchery and sadism in contravention of all military codes going back for centuries. The generals took notice. Murdering all captured Red Army leaders was unthinkable.

Hitler launched Operation Barbarossa on June 22, 1941. The march of the German armies toward Moscow now began. Germany was at war with the Soviet Union. Meanwhile, Oster and Dohnanyi continued their work under the protection of Admiral Canaris. If ever anyone led a double life, Canaris did. He took morning horseback rides in Berlin's Tiergarten with Heydrich, the piscine ghoul, and yet was at this very time using his power to undermine Heydrich and the Nazis at every turn.

With the help of Oster and Dohnanyi, Bonhoeffer got exemptions and deferments for a number of pastors in the Confessing Church. He hoped to keep them from danger, but also to keep them functioning as pastors since the needs of their flocks were greater than ever.

Much of Bonhoeffer's pastoral work was now via correspondence. In August he wrote another circular letter to the hundred or so former ordinands. In it one finds words that shed light on his own death:

> Today I must inform you that our brothers Konrad Bojack, F. A. Preuß, Ulrich Nithack, and Gerhard Schulze have been killed on the eastern front. . . . They have gone before us on the path that we shall all have to take at some point. In a particularly gracious way, God reminds those of you who are out on the front to remain prepared. . . . To be sure, God shall call you, and us, only at the hour that God has chosen. Until that hour, which lies in God's hand alone, we shall all be protected even in greatest danger; and from our gratitude for such protection ever new readiness surely arises for the final call.

Who can comprehend how those whom God takes so early are chosen? Does not the early death of young Christians always appear to us as if God were plundering his own best instruments in a time in which they are most needed? Yet the Lord makes no mistakes. Might God need our brothers for some hidden service on our behalf in the heavenly world? We should put an end to our human thoughts, which always wish to know more than they can, and cling to that which is certain. Whomever God calls home is someone God has loved. "For their souls were pleasing to the Lord, therefore he took them quickly from the midst of wickedness" (Wisdom of Solomon 4).

We know, of course, that God and the devil are engaged in battle in the world and that the devil also has a say in death. In the face of death we cannot simply speak in some fatalistic way, "God wills it"; but we must juxtapose it with the other reality, "God does not will it." Death reveals that the world is not as it should be but that it stands in need of redemption. Christ alone is the conquering of death. Here the sharp antithesis between "God wills it" and "God does not will it" comes to a head and also finds its resolution. God accedes to that which God does not will, and from now on death itself must therefore serve God. From now on, the "God wills it" encompasses even the "God does not will it." God wills the conquering of death through the death of Jesus Christ. Only in the cross and resurrection of Jesus Christ has death been drawn into God's power, and it must now serve God's own aims. It is not some fatalistic surrender but rather a living faith in Jesus Christ, who died and rose for us, that is able to cope profoundly with death.

In life with Jesus Christ, death as a general fate approaching us from without is confronted by death from within, one's own death, the free death of daily dying with Jesus Christ. Those who live with Christ die daily to their own will. Christ in us gives us over to death so that he can live within us. Thus our inner dying grows to meet that death from without. Christians receive their own death in this way, and in this way our physical death very truly becomes not the end but rather the fulfillment of our life with Jesus Christ. Here we enter into community with the One who at his own death was able to say, "It is finished."[3]

Although not on the front lines himself, he heard from many of the brethren who were, encouraging them by return mail and praying for them. One of them, Erich Klapproth, wrote that the temperature was forty below zero: "For days at a stretch we cannot even wash our hands, but go from the dead bodies to a meal and from there back to the rifle. All one's energy has to be summoned up to fight against the danger of freezing, to be on the move even when one is dead tired." Klapproth wondered whether they would ever be allowed to return home again, to resume their calm and quiet lives. Shortly thereafter, Bonhoeffer learned that he had been killed.

By the fall of 1941, all hopes that the conspiracy could get Britain's assurances of a negotiated peace were gone. The war had dragged on too long. With Germany fighting Russia, Churchill, now prime minister, saw it as all or nothing. He was not interested in the conspiracy—if one even existed.

As Germany's armies moved toward Moscow, the barbarism of the SS had again been given the freedom to express itself. It was as if the devil and his hordes had crawled out of hell and walked the earth. In Lithuania, SS squads gathered defenseless Jews together and beat them to death with truncheons, afterward dancing to music on the dead bodies. The victims were cleared away, a second group was brought in, and the macabre exercise was repeated.

As a result of such things, many more in the army leadership were driven to the conspiracy. At one point officers came to Field Marshal Bock and begged him with tears in their eyes to stop "the orgy of executions" in Borisov. But even Bock was powerless. When he demanded that the SS commander in charge of the massacres be brought to him, the civilian commissioner, Wilhelm Kube, laughed defiantly. Hitler had given the SS free rein, and even a field marshal could do nothing about it.

When Bonhoeffer returned from Switzerland in late September, he learned of more horrors. A new decree required all Jews in Germany to wear a yellow star in public. At the Dohnanyis' house that September, Bonhoeffer famously said that, if necessary, he would be willing to kill Hitler. He stipulated, however, that he would first have to resign from the Confessing Church.

Hitler Stumbles

In October, Dohnanyi and Oster met with Fabian von Schlabrendorff and Major General Henning von Tresckow, who believed that things were again ripe for toppling Hitler. The generals on the Russian front were becoming increasingly annoyed with the Führer's interference. Between this and the continuing sadism of the SS, many were finally ready to turn against him.

In November 1941 German troops under the command of Field Marshal von Rundstedt were roaring toward Stalingrad when on November 26 in Rostov, they suffered a serious defeat and began to retreat. It was the first time any of Hitler's forces were decisively routed, and it was not something the Führer's hubris could accommodate. He was personally affronted and now, from a thousand miles away at *Wolfsschanze*, his bunker in the woods of East Prussia, Hitler demanded that Rundstedt hold the line at all costs. His troops must pay any price and bear any burden. Rundstedt wired back that it was "madness" to attempt to do so. "I repeat," Rundstedt continued, "that this order be rescinded or that you find someone else." Hitler relieved Rundstedt of his command and did so.

The tide was turning for Adolf Hitler. The rest of his eastern armies were now charging into the white jaws of the notorious Russian winter, whose fury increased with each day. Thousands of soldiers were dying from severe frostbite. Fuel was freezing. Fires had to be started under tanks in order to start them. Because of the cold, machine guns ceased firing. Telescopic sights were useless.

Still, Hitler mercilessly drove his armies forward, and on December 2, a single German battalion pushed close enough to glimpse the fabled golden spires of the Kremlin, fourteen miles away. That was as close as the Germans would get. On December 4 the temperature fell to thirty-one below zero. On the fifth it fell to thirty-six below zero. On the sixth the Russians attacked the German lines with such shattering force that the once invincible armies of Adolf Hitler turned tail and went into full retreat.

The reversal pierced Hitler like a dagger, but the news on December 7 of the sneaky Japanese attack on Pearl Harbor revived his spirits. He especially rejoiced at the underhandedness of the attack, saying that it corresponded to his "own system," and in that eternally sunny way of his he interpreted the mass murder of Americans as an encouraging sign from Providence, just when he needed one.

A series of generals were replaced, imprisoned, or killed. General Brauchitsch, commander in chief of the German army, responded to the fiasco with coronary failure and turned in his resignation. This was catastrophic for the conspirators, who had been courting Brauchitsch for some time and had lately gotten his assent to their plans. Now their wobbly linchpin had pulled himself out.

The conspirators' plans were roughly the same as before: Hitler would be assassinated. General Beck, who had resigned in protest four years earlier, would lead the coup and likely become the head of a new government. According to Gisevius, Beck "stood above all parties . . . [as] the only general with an unimpaired reputation, the only general who had voluntarily resigned." Having Beck as the leader of a new German government gave many generals the courage to move forward.

Meanwhile the larger conspiracy went ahead on several fronts, with the Abwehr planning to send Bonhoeffer on a mission to Norway in early April. For the first time, though, in February 1942, Dohnanyi learned that the Gestapo was watching him and Bonhoeffer. Dohnanyi's telephone had been tapped, and his correspondence was being intercepted. Martin Bormann and the cadaverous Heydrich were likely behind it. Aware of the increasing danger, Bonhoeffer drew up a will, which he gave to Bethge; he did not want to alarm his family.

Before the end of June, Heydrich was dead. At the end of May, the albino stoat was ambushed by Czech Resistance fighters while he was riding in his open-topped Mercedes. Eight days later, the architect of the Final Solution fell into the hands of the God of Abraham, Isaac, and Jacob.

But the Gestapo did not forget about Bonhoeffer and Dohnanyi.

✛ CHAPTER 10

BONHOEFFER IN LOVE

1942–1943

*Why am I suddenly so cheerful these days? . . . The
incredible fact remains, he actually wants to marry me. I still
fail to grasp how that can be.*

—MARIA VON WEDEMEYER

O
n June 8, 1942, Bonhoeffer went to Klein-Krössin
to visit his dear friend Ruth von Kleist-Retzow. Her
granddaughter Maria happened to be there. She had
just graduated from high school, and before embark-
ing on a year of national service, she had decided to spend some
time visiting family. "Foremost among these visits," she recalled,

was one to my grandmother, to whom I had always been
close. The feeling was mutual, because she thought I resembled her as a young girl. I had been there a week when the
celebrated Pastor Bonhoeffer came to stay. I was a bit put
out at first, to be honest, but it very soon emerged that the

three of us got on extremely well together. The other two conversed in such a way that I not only felt I understood what they were talking about but was cordially encouraged to join in. Which I did.

I'm afraid I used to take a cocky tone with my grandmother, which amused her, and which I maintained even when Dietrich turned up. We talked about future plans. Grandmother pronounced my plan to study mathematics a silly whim, but Dietrich, perhaps for that very reason, took it seriously.

We went for a stroll in the garden. He said he'd been to America, and we noted with surprise that I'd never before met anyone who had been there.[1]

Maria left the next morning, so they didn't have much time together, but Bonhoeffer was smitten. As ever, he needed time to process what he was feeling and thinking. But he was taken aback at how affected he had been by the short time spent with this beautiful, intelligent, and confident young woman. She was eighteen, he was twice that.

Bonhoeffer knew Maria's family well. Besides his abiding friendship with her grandmother, he had spent much time with her brother Max, who was two years her senior and whom she adored. Max was then a lieutenant serving on the eastern front. Bonhoeffer knew her parents, too, Hans and Ruth von Wedemeyer; a couple more devoutly Christian—and anti-Hitler—did not exist.

That week, in the charmed surroundings of Klein-Krössin, Bonhoeffer worked on his book. Whether he and Ruth von Kleist-Retzow spoke about Maria as a potential wife is unknown. It's likely the thought crossed her mind, since she was the most ardent supporter of the union once the couple publicly discussed its possibility. She was also outspoken and strong-willed, and that she suggested the idea to Bonhoeffer cannot be ruled out.

Weeks later, Bonhoeffer spoke to Eberhard Bethge about Maria.

As with anything, he was trying to work out what he thought God was saying to him. On June 25, he wrote Bethge:

> I have not written to Maria. It is truly not time for that yet. If no further meetings are possible, the pleasant thought of a few highly charged minutes will surely eventually dissolve into the realm of unfulfilled fantasies, a realm that in any case is already well populated. On the other side, I do not see how a meeting could be brought off that would be inconspicuous and not painful for her. Even Mrs. von Kleist cannot be expected to arrange this, at least not at my initiation; for I am in fact still not at all clear and decided about this.[2]

On the twenty-seventh, Bonhoeffer flew to Venice with Dohnanyi on Abwehr business. A week later he was in Rome, and on July 10 he was back in Berlin. He planned to be back at Klein-Krössin ten days later, but could not return until August 18. He had had no contact with Maria since their meeting. But now, while he was again in Klein-Krössin, tragedy struck. Maria's father was killed at Stalingrad. He was fifty-four.

Hans von Wedemeyer had been commanding a regiment that, like most at that time, was fatigued and depleted. On the night of August 21, the Russians launched a shell attack, and he was hit. In Hanover, Maria heard of her father's death and immediately traveled home to Pätzig.

Bonhoeffer returned to Klein-Krössin on September 1 for two days, and again for two days on September 22. Neither time did he see Maria. But he saw her on October 2 in Berlin. It was their first meeting since early June.

Ruth von Kleist-Retzow was in Berlin for an eye operation at the Franciscan hospital, and she had asked Maria to nurse her there. At the sickbed of her grandmother, she bumped into Dietrich again. Her thoughts toward him had not been along the lines of his toward her, nor had Bonhoeffer allowed his thoughts to get very far. But, in any case, he was at the hospital in the role of pastor, and Maria had just lost her father.

Years later, Maria recalled, "Dietrich's frequent visits [at the hospital] surprised me, and I was impressed by his devotion. We often had long talks together at this time. It was a reunion under different circumstances than in June. Being still deeply affected by my father's death, I needed Dietrich's help." They spent more time together than would have been possible under other circumstances. As a native Berliner, Bonhoeffer played the role of host. One day he invited Maria to lunch, suggesting they go to a small restaurant near the hospital. He said because of the ownership, it was actually the safest place for them to talk freely. It was owned by Hitler's brother.

On October 15 Bonhoeffer invited Maria to a Bonhoeffer family gathering at his sister Ursula's home. It was a farewell celebration for his nephew Hans-Walter Schleicher, who was heading off to war the next day.

Maria met Bonhoeffer's parents and siblings. Bethge was likely there too. That evening, after returning to her aunt's home, where she was staying, Maria wrote in her diary:

> I had a very interesting talk with Pastor Bonhoeffer. He said it was a tradition with us that young men should volunteer for military service and lay down their lives for a cause of which they mightn't approve at all. But there must also be people able to fight from conviction alone. If they approved of the grounds for war, well and good. If not, they could best serve the Fatherland by operating on the internal front, perhaps even by working against the regime. It would thus be their task to avoid serving in the armed forces for as long as possible—and even, under certain circumstances, if they wouldn't reconcile it with their conscience, to be conscientious objectors.

Oh, it's all so logically clear and obvious. But isn't it terrible, when I think of my father?[3]

Three days later, a Sunday, Bonhoeffer was again at the hospital to visit Ruth von Kleist-Retzow. His sense of propriety and his desire to be a pastoral comfort to Maria must have made it easier to avoid thinking too much about a future with her. Neither seemed to have breathed a word indicating this was more than a family pastor ministering to an older woman and her granddaughter who had just lost her father. And yet they enjoyed each other's company; perhaps the constraints of the situation made it easier to relax with each other.

Then on October 26, fresh tragedy struck. Maria's brother Max was killed. On the thirty-first, Bonhoeffer wrote her:

Dear Miss von Wedemeyer,

If I might be allowed to say only this to you, I believe I have an inkling of what Max's death means for you.

It can scarcely help to tell you I too share in this pain.

At such times it can only help us to cast ourselves upon the heart of God, not with words but truly and entirely. This requires many difficult hours, day and night, but when we have let go entirely into God—or better, when God has received us—then we are helped. "Weeping may endure for the night, but joy comes in the morning" (Psalm 30:5). There really is joy with God, with Christ! Do believe it.

But each person must walk this way alone—or rather, God draws each person onto it individually. Only prayers and the encouragement of others can accompany us along this way.[4]

If ever there was a time to put aside thoughts of a romantic relationship, this was it. Other than his conversations with Bethge, it's doubtful Bonhoeffer mentioned his feelings to anyone. Maria had no such feelings to speak of, and therefore cannot have seen him as more than a friendly and devout pastor friend. It was in that context that Bonhoeffer expected to travel to Pomerania to be at Max's memorial service.

But somehow, Maria's grandmother, who had been watching them from her hospital bed for weeks—and had doubtless noticed their chemistry in June—had other ideas. She foolishly mentioned them to her daughter. Maria's mother now sent Bonhoeffer a letter asking him not to come to the funeral. He was stunned. Frau von Wedemeyer felt her daughter was too young to be engaged to Pastor Bonhoeffer and thought any discussion of it inappropriate at such a time. Bonhoeffer was shocked to think any of this could be in the open. That anyone was discussing these things when he himself had not discussed them was a horror. On the eleventh, after getting the letter from Maria's mother, Bonhoeffer called Ruth von Kleist-Retzow immediately, knowing she had started the trouble.

Maria was blindsided by the whole thing. She wrote Bonhoeffer a letter saying that she had learned that her mother "had asked you not to come for the memorial service, just because of some stupid family gossip which Grandmother has rather encouraged." As far as Maria was concerned, there was nothing to it, except that she was embarrassed.

Bonhoeffer responded:

November 13, 1942

Dear Miss von Wedemeyer,

Your letter has brought a salutary clarity into an unnecessarily confused situation. With my whole heart I thank you for this, as well as for the courage with which you have taken the bull by the horns. You will surely understand that I was unable to find your mother's request entirely comprehensible; what I did understand readily—because it corresponds to my own feelings—was simply the wish not to be worried and burdened by something else altogether in these difficult days and weeks. Whatever else may have spurred her request was not spelled out in the letter, and I had no right to inquire about it. . . .

You, as much as or perhaps even more than I, will perceive as a painful inner burden that things not suitable for discussion were brought out into the open. Let me say openly that I cannot easily quite come to terms with your grandmother's behavior; I told her countless times that I did not wish to discuss such things, in fact that this would do violence to all parties. I believed that it was because of her illness and age that she could not cherish silently in her heart what she believed she was witnessing. My conversations with her were often difficult to endure; she did not heed my request. I then interpreted your premature departure from Berlin within that context and was grieved by it. . . . We must make great effort to bear no hard feelings toward her.[5]

But in this letter, in a sidewise, ever-so-gentle way, Bonhoeffer took the opportunity of this opening up of things, however unintended, to hint his way forward:

. . . only from a peaceful, free, healed heart can anything good and right take place; I have experienced that repeatedly in life, and I pray (forgive me for speaking thus) that God may grant us this, soon and very soon.

Can you understand all this? Might you experience it just as I do? I hope so, in fact, I cannot conceive of anything else. But how difficult this is for you too!

. . . Please forgive me this letter, which says so clumsily what I am feeling. I realize that words intended to say personal things come only with tremendous difficulty to me; this is a great burden for those around me. Your grandmother has often enough reproached me severely for my aloofness;

she herself is so completely different, but people must of
course accept and bear one another as they are. . . . I am
writing your grandmother very briefly, urging her to silence
and patience. I will write to your mother tomorrow, that she
not get upset at whatever your grandmother may be writing;
the thought of it horrifies me.[6]

What Maria really thought after reading his letter is unknown,
but this might have been her first inkling that he had feelings for
her. He wrote her again two days later, on November 15. Frau von
Wedemeyer was displeased about the spate of letters and must have
had unpleasant conversations with her mother and daughter. On
the nineteenth she called Bonhoeffer at his parents' home. She said
Maria did not wish to receive any more letters, although it's as likely
that Frau von Wedemeyer herself had made this decision on her
daughter's behalf. Bonhoeffer wrote Maria later that day:

Dear Miss von Wedemeyer,
        Your mother called me this morning and told me of your
wish. The telephone is a very inadequate means of communication, not least because I was unable to be alone during
the conversation. Please forgive me if I have burdened you
too greatly with my letters. I had not wished this but desired
your peace of mind. It appears—this was how I was obliged to
understand your mother—that at the moment we are unable to
give this to each other. So I ask it of God for you and for us and
will wait until God shows us our way. Only in peace with God,
with others, and with ourselves will we hear and do God's will.
In this we may have great confidence and need not become
impatient or act rashly.
        Do not think I failed to understand that you do not want
to respond and cannot and most likely also did not wish to
receive this letter. But if the timing proves feasible for me to

come again to Klein-Krössin at some point in the not too distant future, your wishes would not forbid this? This is what I understand, in any case.

Please forget every word that hurt you and burdened you further beyond what has already been laid on you by God.

I have written to your mother that I needed to write you briefly once more.—

God protect you and us all.

Sincerely yours,

Dietrich Bonhoeffer[7]

Bonhoeffer Proposes

What happened next is anyone's guess, but the well-meaning grandmother's big mouth had flushed the bird from its hiding place. Suddenly everything was out in the open. On November 24, Bonhoeffer traveled to Pätzig to visit with Frau von Wedemeyer. Somehow, in a thunderclap of time, he had decided he wanted to marry Maria von Wedemeyer. He was going to ask her mother's permission to propose.

Bonhoeffer respected Frau von Wedemeyer, but feared she might be overly pious. He wrote Bethge three days later: "Contrary to my fears that the house would have an excessive spiritual tone, its style made a very pleasant impression." Frau von Wedemeyer was "calm, friendly, and not overwrought, as I had feared." She was not unalterably opposed to the match, but "given the enormity of the decision," she proposed a yearlong separation. Bonhoeffer responded that "these days a year could just as well become five or ten and thus represented a postponement into the incalculable." Nonetheless he told Frau von Wedemeyer that he "understood and recognized her maternal authority over her daughter."

Maria's grandmother promptly blew up on hearing that her daughter would take such a severe stand, and Bonhoeffer realized the feisty Ruth would probably cause more trouble. Bonhoeffer didn't see Maria during his visit, but gathered from her mother that she was generally amenable to the separation, although she obviously had little say in the matter.

During this very same time, Eberhard Bethge proposed marriage to Bonhoeffer's sixteen-year-old niece, Renate Schleicher. Her parents, Ursula and Rüdiger, were concerned about the match for similar reasons, Bethge then being thirty-three. The Schleichers also suggested a lengthy separation. "If it begins to look ominous for you," Bonhoeffer said, ". . . I shall in that case say something about my own situation; then for once they will consider your situation not only from Renate's perspective but also from your own. But for now I shall hold my peace."

Maria's diary three days, a month, and six weeks later shows us the progress of her feelings:

Nov. 27th. Why am I suddenly so cheerful these days? I feel safe, for one thing, because I can now postpone all my musings, deliberations and worries till later. But shelving them surely can't be responsible for this sense of relief. Ever since Mother told me on the phone about her meeting with Dietrich, I feel I can breathe freely again. He made a considerable impression on Mother, that's obvious—he couldn't fail to.

The incredible fact remains, he actually wants to marry me. I still fail to grasp how that can be.[8]

19 December 1942. Pätzig.

I thought coming home might be the one thing that could shake my resolve. I still believed I was under the influence of Grandmother, or rather, of her own exaggerated and unrealistic idea, but it isn't true. The innermost reality still stands, even though I don't love him. But I know that I will love him.

Oh, there are so many superficial arguments against it. He's old and wise for his age—a thoroughgoing academic, I suppose. How will I, with my love of dancing, riding, sport, pleasure, be able to forgo all those things? . . . Mother says he's an idealist and hasn't given it careful thought. I don't believe that.[9]

10 Jan 1943. On the way here I had the talk with Mother, the one I had longed for so eagerly but feared so greatly. It caused tears—hot, heavy tears—"and yet, what happiness to be loved. . . ." Was it good and productive? I pray so, because I feel that it was, and is, crucial to my life. I pray, too, that I didn't just talk Mother round but convinced her—that she isn't just giving in to me but can look upon it as the proper course.[10]

Bonhoeffer had had no communication with Maria since November, but on January 10 she spoke with her mother and uncle Hans Jürgen von Kleist-Retzow, who was her guardian, and persuaded them to allow her to write Bonhoeffer. She wrote on the thirteenth:

Dear Pastor Bonhoeffer,
I've known, ever since arriving home, that I must write to you, and I've looked forward to doing so.
I recently spoke with my mother and my uncle from Kieckow. I'm now able to write to you, and to ask you to answer this letter.
It is so difficult for me to have to put in writing what even in person can scarcely be spoken. I wish to rebut every word that wants to be spoken here, because words are so clumsy and forceful with things that want to be said gently. But because I have experienced that you understand me so well, I now have the courage to write you, although I actually have no right at all to reply to a question you have not even asked me. Today I can say Yes to you from my entire, joyful heart.
Please understand my mother's reluctance to waive the

delay she imposed on us. She still can't believe, from past experience, that our decision will hold good. And I myself am always saddened to think that Grandmother has told you only nice things about me, so you form a false picture of me. Perhaps I should tell you a lot of bad things about myself, because it makes me unhappy to think that you could love me for what I'm not.

But I can't believe that anyone can like me so much for what I really am. I certainly have no wish to hurt you, but I must say this anyway:

If you've realized that I'm not good enough, or that you no longer want to come to me, I beg you to say so. I can still ask you that now, and how infinitely harder it will be if I'm forced to recognize it later on. I myself am quite convinced that I need some more time in which to put my decision to the test, and because I know my time in the Red Cross will be hard, it's essential to me.

This is our business alone, isn't it, not anyone else's. I'm so scared of what other people say, even Grandmother. Can you grant this request?

Thank you from the bottom of my heart for all you've done for me recently. I can only guess how difficult it must have been, because I myself have often found it hard to endure.

Yours, Maria[11]

Bonhoeffer wrote back immediately. For the first time he addressed her by her Christian name, and early in the second paragraph, in the phrase "dear Maria, I thank you for your word," switched to the informal *du*:

Dear Maria,
The letter was under way for four days before just now— an hour ago—arriving here! In an hour the mail is being picked

up again, so at least an initial greeting and thanks must go with it—even if the words I wish to say now have not yet emerged. May I simply say what is in my heart? I sense and am overwhelmed by the awareness that a gift without equal has been given me—after all the confusion of the past weeks I had no longer dared to hope—and now the unimaginably great and blissful thing is simply here, and my heart opens up and becomes quite wide and overflowing with thankfulness and shame and still cannot grasp it at all—this "Yes" that is to be decisive for our entire life. If we were now able to talk in person with each other, there would be so infinitely much—yet fundamentally only always one and the same thing—to say! Is it possible that we will see each other soon? And where? Without having to be afraid of others' words again? Or for one reason or another shall this still not happen? I think now it must happen.

And now I cannot speak any differently than I have often done in my own heart—I want to speak to you as a man speaks to the girl with whom he wants to go through life and who has given him her Yes—dear Maria, I thank you for your word, for all that you have endured for me and for what you are and will be for me. Let us now be and become happy in each other. Whatever time and calm you need to compose yourself, as you write, you must have, in whatever form is good for you. You alone can know that. With your "Yes" I can now also wait peacefully; without the Yes it was difficult and would have become increasingly difficult; now it is easy since I know that you want this and need it. I wish in no way to push or frighten you. I want to care for you and allow the dawning joy of our life to make you light and happy. I understand well that you wish to be entirely alone for a time yet—I have been alone long enough in my life to know the blessing (though, to be sure, also the dangers) of solitude. I understand and understood also throughout these past weeks—if not entirely without pain—that for you it cannot be easy to say Yes to me, and I will never forget that. And it is this, your Yes, which alone can give me the courage as well no longer to say only No to myself. Say no more about the "false image" I could have of you. I want no "image," I want you, just as I beg you with my whole heart to want not an image of me but me myself; and you must know those are two different things. But let us not dwell now on the bad that lurks and has power in every person, but let us encounter each other in great, free forgiveness and love, let us take each other as we are—with thanks and boundless trust in God, who has led us to this point and now loves us.

This letter must be off immediately so that you will receive it tomorrow. God protect you and us both.

Your faithful Dietrich[12]

With that, Dietrich Bonhoeffer was engaged. They would look back on January 17 as the official date.

They were still obliged to wait. Bonhoeffer had much to occupy him. Though he wasn't quite sure of it yet, the Gestapo was on his tail, and the conspiracy was racing forward with yet another plan to kill Hitler.

When six days passed and Bonhoeffer had not heard from Maria, he wrote again, even if it was only to tell her that all was well and that she should not feel rushed. The next day, Sunday the twenty-fourth, he received her letter. She asked him whether they might wait six months before they corresponded. Whether her mother had persuaded her to ask this is not known, and it seemed to surprise Bonhoeffer, but he was too happy to be bothered by much. He was in love.

He asked Maria to inform her grandmother of their new situation and to keep from having any further misunderstandings with the strong-willed woman. The day after Bonhoeffer's thirty-seventh

birthday, he heard from Ruth von Kleist-Restow. Maria had told her
the news.

> You know utterly without saying how I desire to receive you
> fully as a son, when the time comes. That it should still take so
> long is probably the decision of [her] mother and Hans-Jürgen,
> I am *presuming*. Perhaps this is the right thing for M., so that she
> remains quite clear. And if it appears too long for her and you,
> then there will be means and ways to shorten it. What does
> time mean today anyway? . . . Oh, I am happy.
>
> Grandmother[13]

 CHAPTER 11

CELL 92 AT TEGEL PRISON

1942–1945

His soul really shone in the dark desperation of our prison . . .
[Bonhoeffer] had always been afraid that he would not be
strong enough to stand such a test but now he knew there was
nothing in life of which one need ever be afraid.

—Payne Best, in a letter to Sabine

Frau von Wedemeyer's concern about Bonhoeffer was not merely his age; it was also his work for the Abwehr. She might even have known of his involvement in the conspiracy. Drawing an eighteen-year-old girl into a relationship with someone whose future was so uncertain seemed selfish. That Frau von Wedemeyer had just lost her husband and son underscored the uncertainty of things.

Indeed, the Gestapo had stumbled onto Bonhoeffer's trail the previous October. A detail had caught their attention when a customs search officer in Prague discovered a currency irregularity leading to Wilhelm Schmidhuber. Schmidhuber was a member of the Abwehr who visited Bonhoeffer at Ettal in December 1940. The Gestapo wasted no time in finding him. He was interrogated about the smuggling of foreign currency abroad, a grave crime during wartime, even if done under the aegis of the Abwehr. Schmidhuber led them to Bonhoeffer's Catholic friend, Joseph Müller.

It was all greatly troubling, especially when Schmidhuber was transferred to the infamous Gestapo prison on Prinz-Albrecht-Strasse in Berlin. He surrendered information implicating Dohnanyi, Oster, and Bonhoeffer. Bonhoeffer knew he might be arrested and even killed, but he had already come to terms with that reality.

Bonhoeffer's student Wolf-Dieter Zimmermann remembered an extraordinary evening in November 1942. Bonhoeffer was visiting him and his wife at their small house near Berlin. Also there was Werner von Haeften, the younger brother of Hans-Bernd von Haeften, who had been in Bonhoeffer's confirmation class in Grunewald two decades earlier. Werner was deeply involved in the conspiracy. He prodded Bonhoeffer about whether it was permissible to kill Hitler. Zimmermann recalled the conversation:

> Suddenly [Werner] turned to Bonhoeffer and said: "Shall I shoot? I can get inside the Führer's headquarters with my revolver. I know where and when the conferences take place. I can get access." These words frightened us all. They had such an explosive effect that at first each of us endeavored to calm the others down. The discussion lasted for many hours. Bonhoeffer explained that the shooting by itself meant nothing: something had to be gained by it, a change of circumstances, of the government. The liquidation of Hitler would in itself be no use; things might even become worse. That, he said, made the work of the resistance so difficult, that the "there-after" had to be so carefully prepared.[1]

Two Failed Assassinations

In January and February 1943, as the Gestapo gathered information on Bonhoeffer and Dohnanyi, preparations were under way for a coup attempt in March. The Gestapo's noose was tightening, but if the coup succeeded, everyone's problems would be over. The principal players were General Friedrich Olbricht, General Henning von Tresckow, and von Tresckow's aide-de-camp and cousin Fabian von Schlabrendorff, who was married to Maria von Wedemeyer's cousin Luitgard von Bismarck.

On March 13 and March 21, two perfectly executed assassination attempts failed without being detected. It was both disheartening and miraculous. The Resistance had been stymied, but at least it had not been exposed.

Ten days later, the occasion of Karl Bonhoeffer's seventy-fifth birthday was grandly celebrated. Though none of them knew it that day, this was the last, magnificent performance the Bonhoeffer family would give. In some ways it was a fitting and crowning moment for the extraordinary family, for whom such performances had been a tradition over the years. In five days their lives would change dramatically. They would never gather like this again.

But here they were now, singing "Praise the Lord." Everyone was there that day, including their former governess Maria Czeppan and Bethge, who would officially become a member of the family in a month. The only ones missing were the Leibholzes, still in England. But even they managed to make an appearance of sorts, sending a congratulatory telegram through Erwin Sutz.

With exquisite irony, Hitler was represented too. For Karl Bonhoeffer's lifetime of service to Germany, an official from the Reich's Ministry of Culture showed up to award him the nation's coveted Goethe medal. It was presented to him in front of the assemblage, along with a special certificate: "In the name of the German people I bestow on Professor Emeritus Bonhoeffer the Goethe medal for art and science, instituted by the late Reichspräsident Hindenburg. The *Führer*, Adolf Hitler."

The Gestapo Make Their Move

Five days later, on April 5, Bonhoeffer was at home at 43 Marienburgerallee. Around noon, he called the Dohnanyis. Their phone was answered by an unfamiliar man's voice. Bonhoeffer hung up. He knew what was happening: the Gestapo had finally made their move. Bonhoeffer calmly went next door to see Ursula and told her what had happened and what would likely happen next: the Gestapo would arrive and arrest him too. She prepared a large meal for him, and then Bonhoeffer went back home to put his papers in order, since the Gestapo would be having a good look around, as was their habit. He had prepared for this moment for a long time and had even left a few notes specifically for their benefit.

Then he returned to the Schleichers and waited. At four o'clock Bonhoeffer's father came over and told him that two men wished to speak with him. They were upstairs in his room. It was Judge Advocate Manfred Roeder and a Gestapo official named Sonderegger. Bonhoeffer met them, and taking his Bible with him, he was escorted to their black Mercedes and taken away. He would never return.

For the three months between his engagement and his arrest, Bonhoeffer had remained in the midst of a moratorium on communication with Maria. And so in February and March, while the Gestapo was closing in on Bonhoeffer and Dohnanyi, Maria wrote to her fiancé in her diary. On April 5, feeling a deep foreboding, she wrote Dietrich again. "Has something bad happened?" she asked. "I'm afraid it's something very bad." She had had no communication with Bonhoeffer or his family, and had no idea that he had been arrested.

On April 18 she was in Pätzig for the confirmation of her younger brother. By then her feelings about her situation had boiled over, and she had resolved to defy her mother's insistence that she and

Bonhoeffer not see each other. She said as much to her brother-in-law Klaus von Bismarck that day. But a short time after she had done so, she and the Bismarcks returned to the manor house where they spoke with her uncle Hans-Jürgen von Kleist. He knew about Bonhoeffer's arrest and told them of it. It was the first Maria had heard.

Now it was too late to see him. For the rest of her life, Maria regretted not having defied her mother's wishes earlier. Her mother came to regret her actions on this score and reproached herself, and Maria took pains to forgive her.

First Days at Tegel

On the day Bonhoeffer was arrested, they also arrested Dohnanyi and Joseph Müller, who were taken to the Wehrmacht prison on the Lehrter Strasse for ranking officers. Bonhoeffer's sister Christine was arrested, too, as was Müller's wife. Both were taken to the women's prison in Charlottenburg. Bonhoeffer alone had been taken to Tegel military prison.

Months later, Bonhoeffer wrote an account of his first days there:

> The formalities of admission were correctly completed. For the first night I was locked up in an admission cell. The blankets on the camp bed had such a foul smell that in spite of the cold it was impossible to use them. Next morning a piece of bread was thrown into my cell; I had to pick it up from the floor. A quarter of the coffee consisted of grounds. The sound of the prison staff's vile abuse of the prisoners who were held for investigation penetrated into my cell for the first time; since then I have heard it every day from morning till night. When I had to parade with the other new arrivals, we were addressed by one of the jailers as "scoundrels," etc. etc. We were all asked why we had been arrested, and when I said I

did not know the jailer answered with a scornful laugh, "You'll find that out soon enough." It was six months before I got a warrant for my arrest. As we went through the various offices, some NCOs, who had heard what my profession was, wanted now and then to have a few words with me. . . . I was taken to the most isolated cell on the top floor; a notice, prohibiting all access without special permission, was put outside it. I was told that all my correspondence would be stopped until further notice and that, unlike all the other prisoners, I should not be allowed half an hour a day in the open air, although, according to the prison rules, I was entitled to it. I received neither newspapers nor anything to smoke. After forty-eight hours my Bible was returned to me; it had been searched to see whether I had smuggled inside it a saw, razor blades, or the like. For the next twelve days the cell door was opened only for bringing food in and putting the bucket out. No one said a word to me. I was told nothing about the reason for my detention, or how long it would last. I gathered from various remarks—and it was confirmed later—that I was lodged in the section for the most serious cases, where the condemned prisoners lay shackled.[2]

For the first twelve days Bonhoeffer was treated as a felon. The cells around him held men condemned to death, one of whom wept through Bonhoeffer's first night, making sleep impossible. On the cell wall Bonhoeffer read the wry graffito of a previous occupant: "In a hundred years it'll all be over."

From the beginning of his captivity, Bonhoeffer maintained the daily discipline of scriptural meditation and prayer he had been practicing for more than a decade. Once he got his Bible back, he read it for hours each day. By November he had read through the Old Testament two and a half times.

He was at first on the prison's uppermost floor, the fourth, but was soon transferred to the third, to "a cell looking south with a sweeping view across the prison yard to the pine forest." This seven-by-ten cell, number ninety-two, was immortalized in the book *Love Letters from Cell 92.* It featured a plank bed, a bench along one wall, a stool, a necessary bucket, a wooden door with a tiny circular window through which the guards might observe him, and a not-so-small window above his head providing daylight and fresh air. It might have been worse. Bonhoeffer's family lived seven miles south and visited often, providing him with food, clothing, books, and other things.

And his situation would improve on all counts. At first he had to adhere to the strict one-letter-every-ten-days rule, and these letters could be only one page. This chafed at him terribly. But Bonhoeffer quickly ingratiated himself with a number of the guards, who were able to sneak other letters out for him. The happy result was a gushing torrent of epistolary activity far beyond the few "official" letters he wrote on the ten-day cycle. Between November 1943 and August 1944, Bonhoeffer wrote two hundred very crowded pages to his friend Eberhard Bethge alone. His parents would send small gifts of all kinds, including flowers for his birthday, as would Maria. She even brought him a huge Christmas tree in December, though it was too large to put in his cell and remained in the guards' room. She brought him an Advent wreath instead. He would post favorite works of art around, and would have his tobacco.

But Bonhoeffer's outlook did not depend on these amenities. His first letter home painted a picture of his attitude:

> Dear Parents! I do want you to be quite sure that I'm all right.*
> I'm sorry that I was not allowed to write to you sooner, but I
> was all right during the first ten days too. Strangely enough,

---

* The English translation in *Letters & Papers from Prison* is much less emphatic than what the German sentence indicates. The German "Vor allem . . . dir wissen und auch wirklich glauben, das es mir gut geht" is better translated, "Above all, I want you to know and also to really believe that I am doing well."

the discomforts that one generally associates with prison life, the physical hardships, hardly bother me at all.[3]

This letter and many of the letters he wrote were read by Manfred Roeder, the man prosecuting him. Bonhoeffer was writing on two levels: on one level to his parents, but on another to the hostile set of eyes trolling for incriminating evidence. But he was not merely trying to avoid saying anything incriminating: he was also using this and other letters to paint a particular picture for Roeder. He wanted to give Roeder a general framework in which to interpret things Bonhoeffer said during his interrogations.

Cat and Mouse

Because Bonhoeffer and the others knew the Nazis were ignorant of the conspiracy, they continued their multilevel game of deception. The conspiracy was ongoing while they were behind bars, and they knew that any moment Hitler would probably be assassinated and they would be set free.

One reason the Bonhoeffer family could function as such a hotbed of sedition was their formidable intelligence, and their ability to comfortably communicate on several levels at once, with the confidence of being understood as they did so. Now, Bonhoeffer could write letters home knowing that they would be read and understood on two levels. Bonhoeffer knew his parents would know what he wrote to them was written, in part, to fool Roeder—and he trusted them to be able to tease out what was meant for them and what was meant for him. To some extent they had been functioning like this for years.

They had also worked out ahead of time how to communicate if any of them was imprisoned, and they now used these methods. One involved putting coded messages in the books they were allowed to receive. Bonhoeffer got many books from his parents and would send them back when he was finished with them. To indicate there was a coded message in the book, they underlined the name of the book's owner on the flyleaf or inside cover. If *D. Bonhoeffer* was underlined, the receiver knew there was a message.

The message itself was communicated through a series of the tiniest pencil marks under letters on pages in the book. Every three or every ten pages—the number seemed to vary—a barely visible pencil dot would be put under a letter on that page. Ten pages later another letter would be marked with a dot. These marks would begin at the back of the book and proceed toward the front, so in the course of a three-hundred-page book one might have room for a thirty-letter communication. These were usually extremely important and dangerous messages, such as what Dohnanyi had communicated to his interrogator, so that Bonhoeffer could corroborate that information and not get tripped up or caught contradicting something Dohnanyi said. One message was "O. now officially acknowledges the Rome coding card." In this case, "O" referred to Oster. Another one of the coded book messages was: "I'm not certain that the letter with Hans's corrections has been found, but think so." It could all get a bit baroque, but the Bonhoeffers were up to it.

Renate Bethge recalled that she and the other younger ones often had the task of looking for the barely visible pencil markings since younger eyes were much better at seeing them. They would even use a pencil eraser to see whether the marks had been made with a pencil or were merely tiny irregularities in the actual printing of the book. Christopher von Dohnanyi recalled another way they were able to slip messages past the Nazis: "You could take a glass for jam or marmalade . . . there was a double lid. The lid had a double cardboard. Between this cardboard and the metal, my mother and we would cut little rounds, and there we would write the most dangerous things!" Hans von Dohnanyi wrote entire letters in miniature script on this secret circular stationery.

Throughout his eighteen months at Tegel, Bonhoeffer's basic

pose of the simple and idealistic pastor unconcerned with political issues worked well. He played dumb brilliantly, both in the interrogations and in the often long letters that he wrote to Roeder: "I am the last person to deny that I might have made mistakes in work so strange, so new and so complicated as that of the Abwehr. I often find it hard to follow the speed of your questions, probably because I am not used to them."

As the head of the Abwehr, Admiral Canaris did all he could to provide cover for Dohnanyi and Bonhoeffer. But Bonhoeffer had a further advantage at Tegel, and a very significant one. His uncle Paul von Hase was the military commandant of Berlin and therefore was the big boss, high above the top warden at Tegel prison. When the guards at Tegel learned of this, everything changed. It could hardly have been imagined. Von Hase's nephew was a prisoner! It was as if they had a celebrity in their midst. And not only because of his uncle, but because of the great mystery that attended Bonhoeffer's imprisonment. He was a pastor and quite clearly an enemy of the Nazi state. Many of them were quietly against the Nazis, too, so there grew an undeniable fascination with Bonhoeffer. And as they got to know him, they found him genuinely kind and generous— quite shockingly so, for many of them—even to those guards whom others despised.

Bonhoeffer's Tegel Curriculum

Bonhoeffer was soon given privileges in the prison, sometimes because of who his uncle was, but more often because others in the unpleasant environment found him to be a source of comfort to them and wanted him around. They wished to speak with him, to tell him their problems, to confess things to him, and simply to be near him. He counseled some condemned prisoners and some guards too. Bonhoeffer was also allowed time alone in his cell with others, contrary to explicit orders. And he was allowed to spend a time in the sick bay where he functioned much like a prison pastor instead of a prisoner. In general, Bonhoeffer spent quite a bit of time working pastorally at Tegel, so much so that he sometimes felt he was taking too much time away from his own writing and reading.

Nonetheless, the amount of reading and writing that Bonhoeffer did in his eighteen months at Tegel is decidedly impressive. In a letter to Eberhard Bethge, he wrote:

> In a rather haphazard way I've recently been reading a history of Scotland Yard, a history of prostitution, finished the Delbrück—I find him really rather uninteresting in his problems—, Reinhold Schneider's sonnets—very variable in quality, some very good; on the whole all the newest productions seem to me to be lacking the *hilaritas*—"cheerfulness"—which is to be found in any really great and free intellectual achievement. One has always the impression of a somewhat tortured and strained manufacture instead of creativity in the open air. . . . At the moment I'm reading a gigantic English novel which goes from 1500 to today, by Hugh Walpole, written in 1909. Dilthey is also interesting me very much and for an hour each day I'm studying the manual for medical staff, for any eventuality.[4]

The letters to Bethge opened up far more than opportunities to discuss literature. That he could do with his parents and did. But with Bethge he could discuss things he couldn't discuss with anyone else. In his first letter to Bethge, Bonhoeffer let him know that the depression that sometimes plagued him was not an issue. He feared that Bethge must have been concerned about him on this score.

Bonhoeffer had been resigned to missing Eberhard and Renate's wedding the previous May. But when he learned they were expecting a child, Bonhoeffer was sure he would be out in time to preach at the baptism. The child was even named after him, and he was the godfather. As the date drew near, however, he realized that he would not be out in time for this, either. A week later he sent them "Thoughts on the Day of the Baptism of Dietrich Wilhelm Rüdiger Bethge." It is a small masterpiece. In the letter with this essay he wrote, "Please harbor no regrets about me. Martin [Niemöller] has had nearly seven years of it, and that is a very different matter."

Bonhoeffer thought of *Ethics* as his magnum opus. It is the book that he never quite finished. He had worked on it for years, at Ettal and at Klein-Krössin and at Friedrichsbrunn and in his attic bedroom in Berlin. And now he worked on it in his cell at Tegel. In 1943, to Bethge, he said, "I sometimes feel as if my life were more or less over, and as if all I had to do now were to finish my *Ethics*." Although Bonhoeffer never finished it to his satisfaction, it can be seen, along with his *Discipleship* and *Life Together*, as essentially complete,* and as indisputably important in forming a full understanding of Dietrich Bonhoeffer.

The book opens with these lines:

> Those who wish even to focus on the problem of a Christian ethic are faced with an outrageous demand—from the outset they must give up, as inappropriate to this topic, the very two questions that led them to deal with the ethical problem: "How can I be good?" and "How can I do something good?" Instead they must ask the wholly other, completely different question: "What is the will of God?" . . . All things appear as in a distorted mirror if they are not seen and recognized in God.[5]

Love Letters from Cell 92

Bonhoeffer's relationship with Maria was a source of strength and hope for him now. When she learned of his arrest, Bonhoeffer's

---

* Eberhard Bethge edited the surviving manuscript.

future mother-in-law was moved to allow the engagement to be made public. He was very grateful for this kindness. It gave him and Maria more hope that their future together was a reality, soon to come. Everyone was convinced Bonhoeffer would be released quite soon, once Roeder got his questions answered.

In the meantime, on May 23, Maria visited his parents in Berlin, where she was received as Dietrich's fiancée. Maria even spent a long time alone in Bonhoeffer's room. She wrote him the next day from Hanover:

> My dear, dear Dietrich,
>
> You thought of me yesterday, didn't you? I sense how constantly you were at my side, how you went with me through all those unfamiliar rooms to meet all those people, and how everything suddenly seemed familiar, homely, and very dear. I'm so happy about that day in Berlin, Dietrich—so inexpressibly happy and grateful to you and your parents. I think my happiness is so deeply, firmly rooted that sorrow simply can't reach that far, however immense it may sometimes seem.
>
> I like your parents. The moment your mother greeted me I knew I couldn't fail to, and that you're giving me infinitely more than I ever dreamed. Oh, I fell in love with everything. Your house, the garden, and—most of all—your room. I don't know what I wouldn't give to be able to sit there again, if only to look at the ink-blots on your desk pad. Everything has become so real and clear to me since I met you at your parents' home yesterday. The desk where you wrote your books and your letters to me, your armchair and the ashtray, your shoes on the shelf and your favorite pictures. . . . I never thought I could miss you and long for you more than I do, but I've done so twice as much since yesterday.
>
> . . . My dearest Dietrich, every morning at six, when we both fold our hands in prayer, we know that we can have great

faith, not only in each other but far, far above and beyond that. And then you can't be sad any more either, can you? I'll write again soon.

Whatever I think or do, I'm always

Your Maria[6]

In her next letter, on May 30, she marveled that it was a year since their fateful meeting at Klein-Krössin: "So it's really a year ago already. Just imagine, I find it almost incomprehensible that you should be the gentleman who I met at that time, and with who I discussed first names, *Lili-Marlen*,* daisies, and other matters. Grandmother told me what you remembered about it, and I blushed with retrospective horror at all the silly things I said."

At the beginning of June, Roeder granted Bonhoeffer permission to write Maria. After his first letter, she wrote the following:

June 9, 1943

Dearest Dietrich,

You wrote such a lovely letter . . . the very fact that I can expect another one like it in ten days' time puts me in an incredibly good mood. But when I read it I become almost too happy, and I suddenly think I'll have to awaken from this dream and realize that none of it is true, and laugh at myself for ever having dared to presume such happiness. So you see, my happiness is still so much greater than my sadness—you really must believe that. It won't be long before we see each other again, I'm quite certain, and I say that to you and myself night and morning. . . .

You say you want to hear some wedding plans? I've got more than enough. We must become officially engaged as soon

---

* A popular song of the era, especially among the troops. The German military broadcasting station ended with it each night.

as we're together again. Very few of my family are in the know yet. . . . You won't get away without an engagement party, but we'll marry soon after that. I'd like it to be in summer, when Pätzig looks its best. I've always looked forward so much to showing you Pätzig in August especially. What you've seen of it up to now doesn't count. I'd pictured that August in every detail. How I would meet your train, how I would go for walks with you and show you all my favorite places, views, trees and animals, and how much you would like them too, and then we would have a common home there. Don't be depressed and miserable. Think how happy we'll be later on, and tell yourself that perhaps all this had to happen for us to realize how lovely our life will be and how grateful for it we must be. . . . You must start choosing the hymns and texts right away. I'd like "Sollt ich meinem Gott nicht singen"* and the 103rd Psalm. . . . Please fit them in. As for the rest I'm open to persuasion and suggestion. You know Pätzig church, of course. . . .

We'll have a honeymoon, too! Where? And what then? Then, what matters most is that we're happy, the two of us. Nothing else will count for much, will it?

I've requested a transfer to the Augusta Hospital in Berlin, and am now waiting to be posted there. It could happen with the next few days. Being near you would be so much nicer, and I look forward to being able to visit your parents more often. Think how wonderful it will be when you're free again.

My dear Dietrich, if only I could relieve you of even a little of your burden. There's nothing I wouldn't give for a chance to do so. I'm with you every moment, yet so terribly far away, and I long so inexpressibly much to be with you in reality. You know, don't you, that I'm always

Your Maria[7]

---

* "Shall I not praise my God?"

Maria obtained a visitor's permit for June 24, although Bonhoeffer did not know she would be coming. Roeder surprised Bonhoeffer by bringing Maria into the room. Maria wrote years later, "I was brought into the room with practically no forewarning, and Dietrich was visibly shaken. He first reacted with silence, but then carried on a normal conversation; his emotions showed only in the pressure with which he held my hand."

When their time together was over, Roeder took Maria in one direction, while Bonhoeffer had to leave by another door. They hadn't seen each other since November. Now they'd been given these precious moments, and suddenly the visit was over. But just as Maria was about to leave the room, she manifested the independent spirit and strong will for which she was famous: when she looked back and saw her beloved Dietrich leaving through the door across the room, she impetuously, and obviously against the wishes of Roeder, ran back across the room and hugged her fiancé one last time.

It would be the first of seventeen visits. Sixteen of them were between that date and June 27 of the following year, 1944.* Their hopes for an early trial and release were very much alive, and they were constantly thinking about their upcoming marriage.

In October, Bonhoeffer marked six months at Tegel. On November 26, 1943, he was afforded the unique treat of a visit from the four people in the world he loved most: Maria, his parents, and Eberhard Bethge. They came together, and when Bonhoeffer returned to his cell, he was beside himself:

> It will be with me for a long time now—the memory of having the four people who are nearest and dearest to me with me for a brief moment. When I got back to my cell afterwards, I

---

paced up and down for a whole hour, while my dinner stood
there and got cold, so that at last I couldn't help laughing at
myself when I found myself repeating over and over again,
"That was really great!" I always hesitate to use the word
"indescribable" about anything, because if you take enough
trouble to make a thing clear, I think there is very little that
is really "indescribable"—but at the moment that is just what
this morning seems to be.[8]

On February 4, 1944, his thirty-eighth birthday, Bonhoeffer
received a visit from Maria, who unwittingly bore some hard news.
One of the books she passed along to him that day contained a
coded message from his parents: Admiral Canaris had been dismissed from office. The Gestapo and RSHA had achieved what
they had always longed for: they had brought the renegade Abwehr
under their jurisdiction.

As such, the leadership of the conspiracy to assassinate Hitler
was placed in fresh hands. Over the following months, a new group
of conspirators emerged, headed by Colonel Claus von Stauffenberg.

Valkyrie and the Stauffenberg Plot

On June 30, 1944, Paul von Hase, the military commandant of Berlin,
entered the gates of Tegel prison. His purpose? The prisoner in cell
92, Dietrich Bonhoeffer. It was almost as if Hitler had suddenly
showed up for lunch. Bonhoeffer wrote Bethge that it was "most
comical how everyone goes about flapping his wings and—with a
few notable exceptions—tries to outdo everyone else in undignified
ways. It's painful, but some of them are in such a state now that they
can't help it." Incredibly, von Hase stayed for more than five hours.
Bonhoeffer said his uncle "had four bottles of *Sekt* [German cham-
pagne] brought—a unique event in the annals of this place." It was
"most remarkable," Bonhoeffer thought, that his uncle would dare

to take sides, as it were, against the Nazi prosecution and with his prosecuted nephew.

His uncle's bold appearance suggested that the coup was imminent, that Hitler would soon be dead and they could all begin life again. Bonhoeffer already knew things were in motion, but his uncle's visit strongly confirmed it. Von Hase was not only aware of the coup; he was an integral part of it. The plans for this plot, code-named Valkyrie, had been in existence for a year, but events had never been favorable for their execution. Until now.

The conspirators had moved from thinking prudently to simply wanting to act. As Stauffenberg himself said, "It's time now for something to be done. He who has the courage to act must know that he will probably go down in German history as a traitor. But if he fails to act, he will be a traitor before his own conscience."

The final and famous July 20 plot would be led by Stauffenberg, a devout Catholic from an aristocratic family. In late 1943 he told his fellow conspirator Axel von dem Bussche: "Let's get to the heart of the matter: I am committing high treason with all my might and main."

The name Adolf is a contraction of the Old German *Adelwolf*, meaning "noble wolf." Hitler was aware of this etymology, and in his mystical and eerie way, he adopted the Teutonic and totemic symbol of the wolf as his own. In the 1920s he sometimes registered at hotels as Herr Wolf; the Obersalzberg house was bought under that name; and the Wagner children called him "Onkel Wolf."* He named his military headquarters during the Battle of France *Wolfsschlucht* (Wolf's Gorge), and the command post on the eastern front, *Werwolf* (Werewolf). But the most famous of his lupine haunts was his military headquarters in East Prussia, *Wolfsschanze* (Wolf's Lair).

---

* Hitler adored the composer Richard Wagner (1813–83). He met his widow, Cosima, in 1923 and in subsequent years spent much time with Wagner's children and grandchildren at their home in Bayreuth.

On July 19, Stauffenberg was ordered to be at Wolfsschanze the next day for a one o'clock meeting. He knew this was the chance for which he had been patiently waiting. The next morning, July 20, he arose at five, and before he left, he told his brother Berthold, "We have crossed the Rubicon." He drove to the airport with his adjutant, Werner von Haeften, who had spoken for hours to Bonhoeffer about killing the Führer. With them was Stauffenberg's briefcase, containing important papers and, swaddled in a shirt, a plastic bomb. They stopped at a Catholic chapel where Stauffenberg went to pray.

Their three-hour plane ride got them to Rastenberg around ten. They were picked up by a staff car and driven into the gloomy East Prussian woods surrounding Hitler's headquarters. Just before twelve thirty, Stauffenberg asked if he could change his shirt. General Wilhelm Keitel's aide took Stauffenberg to another room where Stauffenberg closed the door, quickly opened his briefcase, unwrapped the bomb, put on the shirt in which it was wrapped, and set the bomb. It would explode in ten minutes. Stauffenberg hurried to Keitel's car and in a moment they arrived at the conference barracks.

By the time Keitel and Stauffenberg entered the room where Hitler was meeting, four of the ten minutes had vanished. Hitler cursorily acknowledged Stauffenberg, who took his place near the Führer, placing the briefcase under the massive oak table at which they all sat. It was just six feet from the Führer's legs, which—unless he moved—would be separated from their ill-tempered master in five minutes.

Stauffenberg excused himself and walked out of the building, fighting the powerful temptation to break into a sprint. Behind him in the room, a presentation continued to drone on until a sentence was prematurely punctuated by an explosion so powerful that Stauffenberg, now about two hundred yards away, saw bluish-yellow flames shoot out the windows, accompanied by some of the high-ranking men who had milliseconds earlier been dully gazing at maps.

The great oaken table was in smithereens. Hair was on fire. The ceiling had descended to the floor. Several men lay dead. But Hitler was fine and dandy, albeit cartoonishly mussed. "It was Providence that spared me," Hitler declared. "This proves that I'm on the right track. I feel that this is the confirmation of all my work." His extraordinary survival amidst this smoke and death was proof positive that he was straddling the very zeitgeist.

A radio microphone was rigged up around midnight, and all Germany heard the voice of the Führer:

> If I speak to you today, I do so for two special reasons. In the first place, so that you may hear my voice and know that I myself am sound and uninjured; and in the second place, so that you may also hear the particulars about a crime that is without peer in German history. An extremely small clique of ambitious, conscienceless, and criminal and stupid officers forged a plot to eliminate me and, along with me, to exterminate the staff of officers in actual command of the German *Wehrmacht.* The bomb, which was planted by Colonel Count von Stauffenberg, burst two yards from my right side. It injured several of my colleagues; one of them has died. I myself am wholly unhurt. . . . The clique of usurpers is . . . an extremely small band of criminal elements who are now being mercilessly exterminated. . . . This time an accounting will be given such as we National Socialists are wont to give. . . . I wish especially to greet you, my old comrades in the struggle, for it has once more been granted me to escape a fate which holds no terrors for me personally, but which would have brought terror down upon the heads of the German people. I see in this another sign from Providence that I must and therefore shall continue my work.[9]

July 20, 1944. Wolfsschanze, East Prussia. Hours after Stauffenberg's bomb fails to kill him, the mysteriously durable Führer poses with Martin Borman (left), Alfred Jodl, and others.

(Getty Images)

The blow to Hitler's ego must have been shattering, and he wouldn't stand for it. He would wipe out every trace of opposition, and torture information from any conceivable source. The wives and children and other family members and friends of anyone connected to this conspiracy would be hunted down, arrested, and sent to concentration camps. The end of the conspiracy had begun.

Aftermath

Listening to the radio in the sick bay on July 21, Bonhoeffer heard the news of the failed assassination attempt. He knew the ramifications. Days later he heard that Canaris had been arrested. He would soon hear more. Werner von Haeften had died bravely, leaping into a hail of bullets intended for Stauffenberg. Stauffenberg died bravely, too, moments later. Just before being executed, he shouted, "Long live sacred Germany!"

Henning von Tresckow and others took their own lives, most of them for fear of revealing the names of others under torture. Before he did so, Tresckow spoke to Schlabrendorff, who recalled his words:

> The whole world will vilify us now, but I am still totally convinced that we did the right thing. Hitler is the archenemy not only of Germany but of the world. When, in a few hours' time, I go before God to account for what I have done and left undone, I know I will be able to justify in good conscience what I did in the struggle against Hitler. God promised Abraham that He would not destroy Sodom if just ten righteous men could be found in the city, and so I hope that for our sake God will not destroy Germany. None of us can bewail his own death; those who consented to join our circle put on the robe of Nessus. A human being's moral integrity begins when he is prepared to sacrifice his life for his convictions.[10]

Everyone remotely involved in the conspiracy was now arrested and interrogated. Most were tortured. On August 7 and 8 the first of the conspirators was subjected to the *Volksgerichtshof* (People's Court), presided over by Roland Freisler, whom William Shirer has called a "vile and vituperative maniac" and "perhaps the most sinister and bloodthirsty Nazi in the Third Reich after Heydrich."

On August 8, Bonhoeffer's uncle General Paul von Hase was sentenced to death by Freisler and hanged that day at Plötzensee prison. He was fifty-nine years old. His wife was arrested, as were the spouses and relatives of many in the conspiracy. On August 22, Hans von Dohnanyi was taken to Sachsenhausen concentration camp. On September 20, the Chronicle of Shame files (henceforth known as the Zossen files) were discovered at Zossen. For Bonhoeffer and Dohnanyi, this was the disaster of disasters. Dohnanyi had been keeping them since 1938, documenting the criminal horrors of the Nazis. The discovery brought everything into the light, and they knew it. The pretense was over.

But the bravery of the men who had stood against the evil regime came to light now too. Many of these beaten and broken men managed to make statements for posterity during their trials, things that must have knocked Freisler and the other devoted Nazis back on their heels. Ewald von Kleist-Schmenzin said that committing treason against Hitler's regime was "a command from God." Hans-Bernd von Haeften said Hitler would go down in the annals of world history as a "great perpetrator of evil." Von der Schulenberg said to the court: "We resolved to take this deed upon ourselves in order to save Germany from indescribable misery. I realize that I shall be hanged for my part in it, but I do not regret what I did and only hope that someone else will succeed in luckier circumstances." And many others made similar statements. Hitler soon forbade further reportage of the trials.

Maria Loses Hope

Even in the months before the failed July 20 assassination attempt, there were signs from Maria that all the waiting and stress was taking a toll. Her letters to Bonhoeffer came further and further apart, and she began suffering from headaches, insomnia, and even fainting fits. According to her sister, Ruth-Alice, there were "many indications that she was going through an emotional crisis." Her relatives noticed that each time she returned from Tegel, she seemed "desperate," as though it was dawning on her that the situation with Dietrich was not getting any better.

In mid-August, Dietrich's parents informed him that Maria had decided to move in with them and help them at their home in Berlin. Ostensibly she was to perform secretarial duties for Dr. Bonhoeffer, whose office was on the first floor of their home.

Dietrich wrote her,

> My dearly beloved Maria,
>
> So now, entirely of your own volition and without my having repeated my request, you've made the big decision to come here and help my parents. I just can't tell you how happy I am. I couldn't believe it at first, when my parents told me, and I still can't quite grasp how it happened or what made it possible. . . . I had just begun to reconcile myself to the idea that you would be recalled to the Red Cross, and that we wouldn't see each other again for ages. Now all that has changed completely, and it's a godsend from my point of view. I'm bound to worry about you during air raids, it's true, but I shall know that you're near me every hour of every day. How wonderful! What a wonderful decision of yours! I'm so grateful to you!
>
> . . . May I beg a very great favor? Help Mama to cope with all her recurrent worries, dearest Maria, and please be very patient with her. That's the best turn you could do me. It may be that the good Lord has sent you to her precisely because she needs an outstanding daughter-in-law at this time, and the better you get to know Mama the more you'll sense that she really wants nothing for herself (*too* little, perhaps!), and that all her wishes, actions and thoughts are centered on others. Let us pray to God you succeed. And then—I shall see you again soon!! Dearest Maria, we must summon up all our strength again and be patient. Let us not lose heart. God has seen to it that the human heart is stronger than any power on earth. Good-bye for now, dearest Maria, and thank you for everything, everything!
>
> I embrace and kiss you tenderly.
>
> Yours, Dietrich[11]

Maria visited Bonhoeffer again on August 23. As things turned out, it would be the last time they ever saw each other. Bonhoeffer wrote to Bethge that day: "Maria was here today, so fresh and at the same time steadfast and tranquil in a way I've rarely seen."

The Gestapo Prison

On Saturday, September 30, Klaus Bonhoeffer saw a car parked near his house. It caused him to turn around immediately and drive away. Klaus was sure the car was a Gestapo car, and if he had gone home, he would have been arrested and taken away, so he drove to Ursula's house on Marienburgerallee, where he stayed overnight. During this painful episode, Ursula succeeded in talking her brother out of suicide, something that, after Klaus had been arrested, tortured, and sentenced to death, she came to regret.

The same Saturday in which Klaus showed up looking for refuge, their cousin, the wife of General Paul von Hase, was released from prison and showed up at their door as well. Von Hase had been executed by the People's Court, and she had nowhere to go. Because of her husband's role in the conspiracy, none of her relatives would take her in, save Ursula and Rüdiger Schleicher.

The next morning, Sunday, the Gestapo arrived and took Klaus away. That Wednesday, the Gestapo came again to Marienburgerallee and arrested Rüdiger. Now two Bonhoeffer brothers and two Bonhoeffer brothers-in-law were imprisoned. That Sunday, October 8, 1944, Bonhoeffer's eighteen months at Tegel came to an end. He was secretly moved to the Gestapo prison on Prinz-Albrecht-Strasse.

Bonhoeffer's four months in the Gestapo prison were markedly different from his time at Tegel. The cells were underground. Bonhoeffer's was eight-by-five feet, and he had no opportunity to see the light of day. There was no prison yard in which to walk, no thrushes to hear sing, and no friendly guards. Admiral Canaris said to him, "It's hell in here." Also there were Carl Goerdeler, Joseph Müller, General Oster, and Judge Sack. Maria's cousin, Fabian von Schlabrendorff, was there too. It seemed that everyone who had been working for the conspiracy was behind bars. Even Eberhard Bethge had been arrested, although he was not being held in this terrible place.

When Bonhoeffer was first interrogated, he was threatened with torture. He was told that the fate of his parents, his other family members, and his fiancée hung on his confession. Nothing leads us to believe he was ever tortured, but his brother Klaus and most of the others were. In his book *They Almost Killed Hitler*, Schlabrendorff wrote of what he himself suffered.

What Dohnanyi endured is another story. His health suffered greatly. During one Allied bombing, he suffered a stroke that caused him to become partially paralyzed and blind. Still, he was accorded no mercy by the Nazis, who knew that he was one of the conspiracy leaders and would do anything to get information from him. His sufferings were such that he persuaded his wife, Christine, to smuggle a diphtheria baccillus into the prison. If he could infect himself with it, he would not be able to be interrogated.

Bonhoeffer could not write to Maria anymore. She made the trek to the prison a number of times, hoping for permission to visit. Each time she was denied. But as harsh as the conditions were, they were not as bad as they might have been. Himmler and the SS knew the war was winding down, and not in Germany's favor, so they were putting out "peace feelers" and knew they could use these prisoners as bargaining chips. Thus they allowed Bonhoeffer to write Maria at Christmas:

19 December 1944
My dearest Maria,
I'm so glad to be able to write you a Christmas letter, and to be able, through you, to convey my love to my parents and

my brothers and sisters, to thank you all. Our homes will be very quiet at this time. But I have often found that the quieter my surroundings, the more vividly I sense my connection with you all. It's as if, in solitude, the soul develops organs of which we're hardly aware in everyday life. So I haven't for an instant felt lonely and forlorn. You yourself, my parents—all of you including my friends and students on active service—are my constant companions. Your prayers and kind thoughts, passages from the Bible, long-forgotten conversations, pieces of music, books—all are invested with life and reality as never before. I live in a great, unseen realm of whose real existence I'm in no doubt. The old children's song about the angels says "two to cover me, two to wake me," and today we grownups are no less in need than children of preservation, night and morning, by kindly, unseen powers. So you mustn't think I'm unhappy. Anyway, what do happiness and unhappiness mean? They depend so little on circumstances and so much more on what goes on inside us. I'm thankful every day to have you—you and all of you—and that makes me happy and cheerful.

Superficially, there's little difference between here and Tegel. The daily routine is the same, the midday meal is considerably better, breakfast and supper are somewhat more meager. Thank you for all the things you've brought me. I'm being treated well and by the book. The place is well heated. Mobility is all I lack, so I do exercises and pace up and down my cell with the window open. . . . I'm glad I'm allowed to smoke! Thank you for thinking of me and doing all you can for me. From my point of view, knowing that is the most important thing of all.

We've now been waiting for each other for almost two years, dearest Maria. Don't lose heart! I'm glad you're with my parents. Give my fondest love to our mother and the

whole family. Here are another few verses that have occurred
to me in recent nights. They're my Christmas greeting to
you, my parents, and my brothers and sisters. . . . In great
love and gratitude to you, my parents, and my brothers and
sisters.

I embrace you.

Yours, Dietrich[12]

✛ CHAPTER 12

ON THE ROAD TO FREEDOM

1945

*No one has yet believed in God and the kingdom of God, no one
has yet heard about the realm of the resurrected, and not been
homesick from that hour, waiting and looking forward joyfully
to being released from bodily existence . . . Death is hell and
night and cold, if it is not transformed by our faith. But that is
just what is so marvelous, that we can transform death.*

—DIETRICH BONHOEFFER,

FROM A SERMON DELIVERED IN LONDON, NOVEMBER 1933

From this point on, the information on Bonhoeffer becomes
scarce. Most of what we know about him during this
four-month period comes from Schlabrendorff. Some of
his account, from the book *I Knew Dietrich Bonhoeffer*, reads
as follows:

I must admit that I was filled with alarm when I caught sight of Dietrich Bonhoeffer. But when I saw his upright figure and his imperturbable glance, I took comfort, and I knew that he had recognized me without losing his composure. . . . The very next morning I was able to have a word with him in the washroom which had facilities for several people, though the rule was that the prisoners were not allowed to speak to one another, and this was normally strictly watched. . . . Dietrich let me know immediately that he was determined to resist all the efforts of the Gestapo, and to reveal nothing of what our friends' fates made it our duty to keep dark. . . . Dietrich Bonhoeffer told me of his interrogations. . . . His noble and pure soul must have suffered deeply. But he betrayed no sign of it. He was always good-tempered, always of the same kindliness and politeness towards everybody, so that to my surprise, within a short time, he had won over his warders, who were not always kindly disposed. . . . Many little notes he slipped into my hands on which he had written biblical words of comfort and hope. He looked with optimism at his own situation too. He repeatedly told me the Gestapo had no clue to his real activities. . . . When Dohnanyi was also delivered to the Prinz-Albrecht-Strasse prison, Dietrich even managed to get in touch with him. When we returned after an air-raid warning from our cement shelter, his brother-in-law lay on a stretcher in his cell, paralyzed in both legs. With an alacrity that nobody would have believed him capable of, Dietrich Bonhoeffer suddenly dived into the open cell of his brother-in-law. It seemed a miracle that none of the warders saw it. But Dietrich also succeeded in the more difficult part of his venture, in emerging from Dohnanyi's cell unnoticed and getting into line with the column of prisoners who were filing along the corridor. That same evening he told me that he had agreed with Dohnanyi upon all essential points of their further testimony. . . .

On the morning of 3rd February 1945 an air raid turned the city of Berlin into a heap of rubble; the buildings of the Gestapo Headquarters were also burnt out. Tightly squeezed together we were standing in our air-raid shelter when a bomb hit it with an enormous explosion. For a second it seemed as if the shelter were bursting and the ceiling crashing down on top of us. It rocked like a ship tossing in the storm, but it held. At that moment Dietrich Bonhoeffer showed his mettle. He remained quite calm, he did not move a muscle, but stood motionless and relaxed as if nothing had happened.

On 7th February 1945 in the morning I spoke to him for the last time. On the same day around noon the number of his cell was called up amongst others. The prisoners were divided into two groups. Bonhoeffer was transported to Buchenwald, the concentration camp near Weimar.[1]

Buchenwald

In the early afternoon of February 7, Bonhoeffer and a number of other prominent prisoners were taken from their cells and made to wait near two vans that would take them to the concentration camps at Buchenwald and Flossenbürg. There were twenty men, all principal figures in the conspiracy.

Bonhoeffer had just celebrated his thirty-ninth birthday in a Gestapo cell and now saw his first daylight in four months. For most it had been far longer. Wherever they were headed, to be outdoors in this extraordinary company lifted everyone's spirits. It was clear the war was ending and Hitler was finished.

When it was time to board the van, Bonhoeffer and Müller were handcuffed. Bonhoeffer protested in vain. Müller, who had suffered a thousand times worse, offered a word of encouragement to his friend and fellow believer: "Let us go calmly to the gallows as Christians," he said. Bonhoeffer was an ambassador in chains.

Now he would take a long journey, two hundred miles south to Buchenwald.

Buchenwald was one of the Nazi centers of death.* But it was not merely a place where people died; it was a place where death was celebrated and worshiped. Buchenwald and its equivalents throughout the Third Reich were living embodiments of the satanic worldview of the SS, where weakness was preyed upon and crushed. Human beings were sometimes murdered for their skin, which was used to make souvenir items such as wallets and knife cases for members of the SS. The heads of some prisoners were shrunken and given as gifts. Bonhoeffer had heard of these abominable practices through Dohnanyi, but few other Germans knew of them at this time.

Bonhoeffer spent seven weeks at Buchenwald. He was not in the main compound, but just outside it in the cold makeshift prison cellar of a yellow tenement-style building constructed to house Buchenwald staff. It was five or six stories high, and its dank cellar had previously been used as a military jail for the SS. Now it would hold more illustrious prisoners, seventeen of them, in twelve cells.**

We have no letters from Bonhoeffer during this period, but one of the men he met at Buchenwald, the British intelligence officer Captain S. Payne Best, wrote an account of his years in German captivity titled *The Venlo Incident*. From this book we get most of the information about Bonhoeffer's last two months. Best arrived at Buchenwald on February 24, with three other prisoners. One was another British officer, Hugh Falconer; the second was Vassily

---

* The name Buchenwald means "Beech Forest." Though it was not an extermination camp per se, 56,545 people were killed there through forced labor, shooting, hanging, or medical experiments before the Allies liberated it in April 1945.

** Cells 1, 2, 3, 4, 6, 7, and 8—all on one side of the cellar—were very small. Cell 5, also on that side, was about twice as large as the others. On the opposite side were cells 9, 10, 11, and 12, also twice as large as the smaller cells. Between the two rows of cells were two brick walls with one opening between them, so that each of the two rows of cells opened onto a corridor, and there was a central corridor between them, leading to the cellar entrance.

Kokorin, a Soviet air force officer and nephew of Stalin's protegé Molotov; the third was General Friedrich von Rabenau, who joined Bonhoeffer in his small cell.

The sixty-year-old Rabenau was a Christian whose faith had led him to oppose Hitler early on. We know from Dr. Hermann Pünder, who shared the small cell next to theirs, that Rabenau continued to work on his autobiography at Buchenwald, and it seems likely that Bonhoeffer was writing, too, though nothing survived. We also know from Pünder that Rabenau and Bonhoeffer spent hours discussing theology. They also played chess on a set given to Rabenau by Payne Best.

By many degrees the strangest of all who shared the last two months of Bonhoeffer's life were Dr. Waldemar Hoven and Dr. Sigmund Rascher, two of the most evil characters in the Third Reich. When Bonhoeffer arrived, Hoven was a prisoner, but in three weeks, because of a shortage of doctors, he was set free. As the chief doctor at Buchenwald, Hoven had overseen the killings of many inmates, some sick and some healthy.

The thirty-six-year-old Rascher took Hoven's place around February 28. Best met him in the lavatory one morning, "a little man with a ginger moustache" who was "a queer fellow; possibly the queerest character which has ever come my way." Rascher told Best that he had "planned and supervised the construction of the gas chambers and was responsible for the use of prisoners as guinea pigs in medical research." Why Rascher was there is unclear. He had been on Himmler's personal staff and was chief "medical officer" at Dachau. Rascher's principal claims to infamy are his "experiments" on human subjects.

We may assume that over the course of his two months, Bonhoeffer had contact with most of the prisoners. Best described Bonhoeffer as "all humility and sweetness; he always seemed to me to diffuse an atmosphere of happiness, of joy in every smallest event in life, and of deep gratitude for the mere fact that he was alive. . . .

He was one of the very few men that I have ever met to whom his God was real and ever close to him."

Both Falconer and Best remarked on the bickering and mistrust that went on among the other Germans. Best wrote:

> When I first made contact with the other prisoners what struck me most forcedly was the intense distrust of most of the Germans of each other; almost every one of them warned me to be careful of some other as he was a Gestapo spy. . . . This atmosphere of suspicion was typical of Nazi Germany, though it seemed to me strange that these people imprisoned by the Gestapo, had so little inclination to form a common front and pull together.[2]

Bonhoeffer and everyone else hung on in the cold and hunger, knowing that any moment they might be either liberated or killed. At one point they got news about the war's progress that made them realize the Americans were indeed close. The guards were so nervous that they let prisoner General von Falkenhausen listen to the daily war bulletins on the guard room radio, so he could explain to them, with his extraordinary military mind, just how close Germany was to defeat.

March 30, 1945, was Good Friday. On April 1, Easter, the thunder of the American guns could be heard in the distance. They were someplace across the Werra River. Sometime that day the chief guard told the prisoners to get ready to leave. Few had many belongings to carry. Best, however, had a typewriter, a suitcase, and three large boxes.

On the afternoon of Tuesday, April 3, it was announced that they would leave within the hour. Hours passed. At ten that evening, word came. They would not have to travel on foot, but the van that would carry them was designed to accommodate eight people without luggage. They were sixteen and had luggage. The van was fueled by wood fed into a generator, so much of the front section of the van was filled with wood. Once under way, the passenger area became filled with choking wood smoke.

Nonetheless, they were leaving Buchenwald.

Journey into the Unknown

The sixteen prisoners—an oddball crew by any standard—crammed themselves into the van along with their luggage.* Many of them were literally unable to move an inch. It was quite an assemblage: bemedaled and aristocratic army generals, a naval commander, a diplomat and his wife, a depressed Russian air force officer, a Catholic lawyer, a theologian, a woman of questionable morals, and a concentration camp "doctor." As soon as they all got into the van and the back door was locked, the air-raid alert sounded. The guards abandoned them and hightailed it to a safer place, as far from the cellar and its stores of munitions as their legs could carry them. The prisoners waited in the back of the van in the blackness, not knowing whether they would be hit by a bomb. Finally the all clear was sounded, and the military personnel returned and started the engine. The van moved a hundred yards and halted. The wood-fueled engine continued to idle, and within moments the van was filled with fumes, which they inhaled, prompting the man who had helped design the gas chambers to cry out: "My God, this is a death van; we are being gassed!"

They left sometime after ten and traveled through the night, joggling along at fifteen miles per hour, covering eight or nine miles every hour because every hour they stopped to clean the flues and restock the generator with wood.

They had been on the road for some seven or eight hours, and

---

* Payne Best's account says sixteen, although it's unclear who was missing from the original seventeen prisoners.

had in their fits and starts traveled about a hundred miles. The prisoners still had no idea where they were headed. Much of the wood had been consumed, and "by the exercise of great ingenuity," Hugh Falconer had managed to repack things so that they had much more room than before. The guards gave them two loaves of bread and a large wurst, which they divided. There was even something to drink. After thirteen hours of this travel, it was noon and they had reached Weiden, a small town of about thirty thousand in northern Bavaria. Flossenbürg lay ten miles east.

In Weiden they stopped at the police station, and the guards went in. Upon returning, the friendlier of the three told his captives: "You will have to go farther. They can't take you here. Too full." But what did that mean? Dr. Rascher pronounced them all unlikely to be marked for death. Flossenbürg, he said, was never so full that it wouldn't bend the rules to welcome another load of corpses. It was only for living, breathing prisoners that it could be "too full." So this was good news. It seemed they wouldn't be killed that day.

The guards got back in and continued southward. Just as they reached the edge of town, a car passed them and motioned for them to pull over. Two policemen stepped out, and one opened the door of the van. What happened next is unclear, but it seems that perhaps Flossenbürg had room for three prisoners after all. Liedig's and Müller's names were barked, so they gathered their things and got out. For some reason Gehre got out as well. Payne Best's account said that Gehre was called along with Liedig and Müller. Perhaps Gehre wished to stick close to Müller, with whom he'd shared a cell and to whom he'd grown close. In any event, Gehre, Liedig, and Müller bade good-bye to their companions and went with the policemen. It was now Wednesday afternoon, April 4. Best wrote:

> After leaving Weiden there was a marked change in the attitude of the three SS guards. They had obviously left Buchenwald with orders to take us to Flossenbürg, and for so

long they had felt themselves constricted by the sense of an authority guiding them. When Flossenbürg refused to receive us they were apparently sent off on vague instructions to continue a southward course until they found some place where they could deposit us, and so, in a measure, they felt that they shared our lot and like us were just sailing along into the blue with no certain destination.[3]

Sometime that afternoon they stopped in front of a farmhouse. The men took turns outside at the pump. What a strangely jolly scene it must have been, these august figures weary from hunger and lack of sleep standing outside in the sunshine around the pump.

The farmer's wife emerged carrying several loaves of rye bread and a jug of milk. Best said that it was "real good rye bread such as none of us had tasted for years." And then back into the van, which was much roomier now. Several of them could take a nap.

After about six hours, they had gone fifty miles, and as the daylight began to wane, they found themselves approaching the town of Regensburg. The van wandered around in the city, stopping again and again as the guards tried to find a place for their passengers to spend the night. Time and again they failed, got back in the van, and drove on.

After dark they ended up at the main entrance to the state prison. This time the guards opened the van doors and told everyone to get out. When they climbed the stairs into the building, one of the prison guards began ordering them uncivilly, prompting one of their own guards to interrupt him, explaining that they were not ordinary prisoners, but special prisoners who must be treated with courtesy. "Oh!" said a Regensburg guard. "More aristocrats! Well, put them with the other lot on the second floor." As seemed to be the case everywhere, things were very tight. The men slept five to a cell, with three straw mattresses covering the cell floor.

In the morning the cell doors were opened and the men allowed

down the corridor to the lavatory. But what a sight they saw: crowding
the entire corridor were men, women, and children, all family members of the men who were executed and arrested in the Stauffenberg
plot. In fact, a number of Stauffenberg's family were here.*

Best found himself being introduced to this one and that one so
that it seemed more like a festive reception than a line to use the
bathroom in a prison. The German aristocrats all seemed to know one
another or to be related. It seemed that the inmates had taken control
of the prison. They wanted to continue talking with each other and
would not return to their cells. Eventually the guards only managed
to lure them back with breakfast.

In a short time, the air-raid siren sounded, and everyone had to
be let out again and taken into the prison basement. Best said that
"the fun started again" with everyone talking and catching up, putting together pieces of their individual puzzles.

Around five that afternoon, one of the guards who had driven
the van from Buchenwald showed up and declared it was time to
leave. The fourteen Buchenwald prisoners gathered their things,
said their good-byes, and went down to their van again. Everyone's
spirits were considerably improved as they again headed southeast
out of Regensburg, along the Danube.

But no sooner were they a few miles outside of town than the van
violently lurched—and stopped dead. Hugh Falconer was an engi-
neer, and the guards prevailed upon him for his opinion. The steer-
ing was broken. Falconer pronounced it irreparable. When a lonely
bicycle approached them from the opposite direction, the guards
stopped the rider and asked that he inform the police in Regensburg,
so they could send another van. The bicyclist said he would and
pedaled off into the distance. Darkness descended and it got cold.

---

* The Countess Nina von Stauffenberg, pregnant with their fifth child, had been
  arrested immediately after her husband's death on July 20. Their four children had
  been taken to an orphanage and given different names. Their mother gave birth to her
  fifth child while imprisoned.

Hours passed. Best said that the guards were quite miserable and seemed frightened, now behaving more like "comrades in distress." No one ever came.

Finally dawn arrived. The guards opened the doors of the van so everyone could get out. At last a motorcycle appeared. The guards wouldn't take any chances, so one of them rode on the back of it into Regensburg. It was the morning of April 6, the Friday after Easter.

Help arrived at eleven o'clock, in the form of a huge bus with large plate-glass windows and comfortable upholstered seats. The bus came with its own detail of about ten machine-gun-toting SD men.* The three Buchenwald guards remained with the expired green heap.

In about an hour they were in Straubing. The landscape grew hillier and more wooded, and the roads more winding and narrow. Some village girls flagged them down and asked for a lift. When they asked the guards who the prisoners were, they told the girls that they were a film company, on their way to shoot a propaganda film. What was true and what was not true at this point was difficult to say. No one knew where they would sleep or whether they would ride all night. They were heading east, past the Mettin monastery. They hadn't eaten in more than twenty-four hours. Best spied a possibility:

> The country seemed to be strong on poultry, and so many hens wanted to cross the road that our driver had quite a job dodging them, though we rather hoped that one might meet with an accident—we would all have enjoyed some nice roast fowl. I suggested to one of our guards that perhaps we might stop and see if we could beg some eggs at one of the farms, and the idea received immediate approval, but when the guard returned with a capful of eggs we got none and were left to tighten our belts and hope that we were approaching our next meal.[4]

---

* The SD was a separate arm of the SS.

In the early afternoon they came to the small Bavarian village of Schönberg and stopped in front of the village school, a squarish white building of four stories. They had reached their destination. As it happened, the large group of aristocrats that they had left behind in Regensburg had already arrived here. So the number of political prisoners was 150.

Bonhoeffer and his fellow prisoners were taken into the school and shown into a large room on the first floor. This was to be their common cell. The room had been a girls' infirmary and was set up with rows of feather beds with bright blankets. It was all very cheering. Best said that despite the "fatigue and hunger we were all in the highest spirits, nervous, excited, and almost hysterical in our laughter." There were large windows on three sides of the room, so that everyone could look out and drink in the green scenery of the valley. Each person chose his bed. Bonhoeffer took a bed next to Kokorin. In the giddy spirit of the moment everyone wrote his name above his bed, "with humorous comments devised by Rascher."

Bonhoeffer sunned himself at one of the windows, praying and thinking. He spent time talking with Pünder and spent time with Kokorin. They even exchanged addresses. Bonhoeffer still had a few books with him: a volume of Goethe, a Bible, and *Plutarch's Lives*.

After their initial settling in, they became aware of their hunger and banged on the door of their room till a guard arrived. There was no food to be had in the town. There was food in Passau, but Passau was twenty-five miles away, and for such a trip they would need petrol, of which they had none. There was nothing to do but go to sleep.

When they awoke the following day, there was no breakfast. At some point some kind soul from the village who had heard of the "special prisoners" and their predicament sent over potato salad and two large loaves of bread. This was all the food they would have that day, and it was likely the last food Bonhoeffer ever ate. It was Saturday, April 7.

Hugh Falconer wrote to Gerhard Leibholz in Oxford that fall:

[Bonhoeffer] was very happy during the whole the time I knew him, and did a great deal to keep some of the weaker brethren from depression and anxiety. He spent a good deal of time with Wasily Wasiliew Kokorin, Molotov's nephew, who was a delightful young man although an atheist. I think your brother-in-law divided his time with him between instilling the foundations of Christianity and learning Russian.[5]

Bonhoeffer's Last Day

The next day, April 8, was the first Sunday after Easter. In Germany it is called Quasimodo Sunday.* Dr. Pünder asked Bonhoeffer to hold a service for them. Pünder was Catholic, as were a number of others. This, and the fact that Kokorin was an atheist, caused Bonhoeffer to demur. He didn't wish to impose. But Kokorin himself insisted.

So less than twenty-four hours before he left this world, Bonhoeffer performed the offices of a pastor. He prayed and read the verses for that day: Isaiah 53:5 ("With his stripes we are healed") and 1 Peter 1:3 ("Blessed be the God and Father of our Lord Jesus Christ! By his great mercy we have been born anew to a living hope through the resurrection of Jesus Christ from the dead" RSV). He then explained these verses to everyone. Best described the service:

[He] spoke to us in a manner which reached the hearts of all, finding just the right words to express the spirit of our imprisonment and the thoughts and resolutions which it had brought. . . .

---

* The term *Quasimodo Sunday* comes from the two Latin words (*quasi* meaning "as if" and *modo* meaning "in the manner of") that begin the *introit* of the Roman Catholic Mass for that day. They are taken from 1 Peter (2:2: "as newborn babes . . .") and literally mean "as in the style of" or "as in the manner of." Victor Hugo's eponymous hunchback of Notre Dame was named Quasimodo because he was supposedly born on that Sunday in the church calendar.

He had hardly finished his last prayer when the door opened and two evil-looking men in civilian clothes came in and said:

"Prisoner Bonhoeffer. Get ready to come with us." Those words "Come with us"—for all prisoners they had come to mean one thing only—the scaffold.

We bade him good-bye—he drew me aside—"This is the end," he said. "For me the beginning of life."[6]

Bonhoeffer asked Best to remember him to Bishop Bell. Six years later, in a letter to the Bonhoeffer family, Best recalled what he had written about Bonhoeffer in his book, where he had said that he "was a good and saintly man." But in the letter he went further: "In fact my feeling was far stronger than these words imply. He was, without exception, the finest and most lovable man I have ever met."

Bonhoeffer's family had not heard of him since he had left the Gestapo prison two months earlier, so to leave some clue of his whereabouts, he took a blunt pencil and wrote his name and address in the front, middle, and back of the volume of Plutarch— the one his family had given him for his birthday two months earlier—and left it behind. One of Carl Goerdeler's sons who was at the schoolhouse took the book and gave it to the Bonhoeffers years later. Bonhoeffer had been with Goerdeler in the last days before his execution in Berlin, and now, when he ran down the stairs of the schoolhouse to enter the van that would take him to his own execution, he bumped into Goerdeler's widow, who bade him his final friendly good-bye.

Bonhoeffer was on his way to Flossenbürg. The journey that Sunday afternoon was about a hundred miles in a north-northwesterly direction. He had his volume of Goethe with him.

Bonhoeffer's sentence of death was almost certainly by decree of Hitler himself, as were the death sentences of Oster and Dohnanyi. Even Hitler must have known that all was lost for him and for Germany, but he was accustomed to diverting exceedingly precious resources of time, personnel, and gasoline for the purposes of his own revenge.

Bonhoeffer arrived at Flossenbürg sometime late on Sunday. The camp doctor at Flossenbürg was H. Fischer-Hüllstrung. He had no idea whom he was watching at the time, but years later, he gave the following account of Bonhoeffer's last minutes alive:

> On the morning of that day between five and six o'clock the prisoners, among them Admiral Canaris, General Oster, General Thomas and *Reichgerichtsrat* Sack were taken from their cells, and the verdicts of the court martial read out to them. Through the half-open door in one room of the huts I saw Pastor Bonhoeffer, before taking off his prison garb, kneeling on the floor praying fervently to his God. I was most deeply moved by the way this lovable man prayed, so devout and so certain that God heard his prayer. At the place of execution, he again said a short prayer and then climbed the steps to the gallows, brave and composed. His death ensued after a few seconds. In the almost fifty years that I worked as a doctor, I have hardly ever seen a man die so entirely submissive to the will of God.[7]

EPILOGUE

T wo weeks later, on April 23, the Allies marched into Flossenbürg. In another week Hitler committed suicide, and the war was over. At that point neither Maria nor anyone in Bonhoeffer's family knew what had become of him. His sister Sabine did not hear about her twin brother's death until May 31:

Pastor [Julius] Rieger telephoned to us from London and asked whether we were home because he had something to say to us. Gert's reply on the telephone was "We would be very glad to see you."

Soon from the window I saw our friend arriving at the house. The moment I opened the door to him I felt fear. The expression of his face was so pale and drawn that I knew that something serious had happened. We quickly entered the room where Gert was, and then Pastor Rieger said with deep sadness, "It's Dietrich. He is no more—and Klaus too. . . ."[1]

That July, after they had learned of the deaths of their son Klaus and their son-in-law Rüdiger Schleicher, Karl and Paula Bonhoeffer wrote to Sabine and Gert. Communication between Berlin and the

outside world had been nearly impossible. They had heard Dietrich
had been killed, but had not had any confirmation of it yet.

23rd July 1945
My dearest children,
    We have just been told that an opportunity has arisen for
us to send you our greetings and news. It is now three years,
I believe, since we received the last letters from you. Now we
have just heard that Gert sent a telegram to Switzerland in
order to obtain news of the fate of our dear Dietrich. From
this we conclude that you are all still alive, and that is a great
consolation for us in our deep sorrow over the fate of our dear
Klaus, Dietrich and Rüdiger.
    Dietrich spent eighteen months in the military prison at
Tegel. Last October he was handed over to the Gestapo and
transferred to the SS prison in Prinz-Albrechtstrasse. During
the early days of February he was taken from there to various concentration camps such as Buchenwald and Flossenbürg
near Weiden. We did not know where he was.
    His fiancée, Maria von Wedemeyer, who was living with
us at this time, attempted to find out for herself where he was.
But in this she was unsuccessful. After the victory of the Allies
we heard that Dietrich was still alive. But later we received
news that he had been murdered by the Gestapo a little before
the Americans arrived.[2]

Meanwhile, in consultation with Gerhard and Sabine, Pastors
Rieger and Hildebrandt and Bishop Bell organized a memorial service for Dietrich and Klaus Bonhoeffer, which would be held on
July 27 at Holy Trinity Brompton Church, London. Bishop Bell
had asked their permission to broadcast it in Germany as well, and
they agreed. Bishop Bell wrote Sabine and Gert two days before
the service:

The Palace, Chichester 25th July 1945

My dear Sabine, (If I may thus call you.) I am deeply grateful for your letter. All you say, so undeserved, is a great comfort to me; and I am very happy to have Dietrich's photograph. You know something, I am sure, of what his friendship and love meant to me. My heart is full of sorrow for you, for alas, it is only too true that the gap he and Klaus leave can never be filled. I pray that God may give peace and strength to your parents, and to all who mourn, and bless them.[3]

The memorial service at Holy Trinity Brompton that July 27, to which the Bonhoeffer parents listened in their home at 43 Marienburgerallee, began with the familiar English hymn, "For All the Saints." The congregation sang the hymn's seven stanzas, and then Bishop Bell prayed the prayer of supplication and the prayer of thanksgiving. Another hymn, "Hark, a Herald Voice Is Calling," was sung in English and in German. Then the gospel lesson was read. Appropriately enough, it was from the Sermon on the Mount.

In her recollection of the service, Sabine said:

The choir of the community to which Dietrich had formerly ministered gave a particularly beautiful rendering of *Wer nur den lieben Gott lässt walten* (Who makes the will of God his only rule), and later we all sang together the hymn which Dietrich had arranged to be sung the last time he preached in London: *Mir nach, spricht Christus, unser Held* (Follow me, says Christ, our hero).[4]

After that Bishop Bell preached:

He was quite clear in his convictions, and for all that he was so young and unassuming, he saw the truth and spoke it out with absolute freedom and without fear. When he came to me all unexpectedly in 1942 at Stockholm as the emissary of the

Resistance to Hitler, he was, as always, absolutely open and
quite untroubled about his own person, his safety. Wherever
he went and whoever he spoke with—whether young or old—
he was fearless, regardless of himself and, with it all, devoted
his heart and soul to his parents, his friends, his country as
God willed it to be, to his Church and to his Master.[5]

Bell ended his sermon with the words, "The blood of martyrs is
the seed of the Church." Julius Rieger and Franz Hildebrandt also
spoke.

Franz Hildebrandt's sermon ended thus:

We know not what to do. After these anxious weeks of uncertainty through which we have lived with you, dear Sabine and
Gert, and with your parents, we know less than ever how to
carry on without the counsel of our brother on whom we could
lean and who was so desperately needed by the Church at this
time. Today we understand what Harnack said when Holl had
died: "with him a piece of my own life is carried to the grave."
Yet: our eyes are upon Thee. We believe in the communion
of saints, the forgiveness of sins, the resurrection of the body
and the life everlasting. We give thanks to God for the life, the
suffering, the witness of our brother whose friends we were
privileged to be. We pray God to lead us, too, through his
discipleship from this world into His heavenly kingdom; to
fulfil in us that other word with which Dietrich concluded his
obituary of Harnack: *"non potest non laetari qui sperat in Dominum"*—
"while in God confiding I cannot but rejoice."[6]

When the service ended, Karl and Paula Bonhoeffer turned off
the radio.

NOTES

CHAPTER 1: FAMILY AND CHILDHOOD

1. Mary Bosanquet, *The Life and Death of Dietrich Bonhoeffer* (New York: Harper and Row, 1968), 24.
2. Ibid., 29.
3. Eberhard Bethge, *Dietrich Bonhoeffer: A Biography*, rev. ed. (Minneapolis: Augsburg Fortress, 2000), 22.
4. Sabine Leibholz-Bonhoeffer, *The Bonhoeffers: Portrait of a Family* (New York: St. Martin's Press, 1971), 4.
5. Renate Bethge and Christian Gremmels, eds., *Dietrich Bonhoeffer: A Life in Pictures*, trans. Brian McNeil (Minneapolis: Fortress Press, 2006), 28.
6. Wolf-Dieter Zimmermann and Ronald G. Smith, eds., *I Knew Dietrich Bonhoeffer*, trans. Käthe Gregor Smith (New York: Harper and Row, 1966), 24.
7. Leibholz-Bonhoeffer, *The Bonhoeffers*, 22–23.
8. Ibid., 21–22.
9. Bethge, *Dietrich Bonhoeffer: A Biography*, 27.
10. Zimmerman and Smith, *I Knew Dietrich Bonhoeffer*, 36.

CHAPTER 2: BONHOEFFER THE STUDENT

1. *The Young Bonhoeffer: 1918–1927*, vol. 9, *Dietrich Bonhoeffer Works*, trans. and ed. Hans Pfeifer et al. (New York: Fortress Press, 2002), 78.
2. Ibid., 106–07.
3. Ruth-Alice von Bismarck and Ulrich Kabitz, eds., *Love Letters from Cell 92: The Correspondence Between Dietrich Bonhoeffer and Maria Von Wedemeyer, 1943–45*, trans. John Brownjohn (New York: Abingdon Press, 1995), 246.

CHAPTER 3: BETWEEN THE PULPIT AND THE LECTERN

1. *Barcelona, Berlin, New York: 1928–1931*, vol. 10, *Dietrich Bonhoeffer Works*, ed. Clifford J. Green, trans. Douglas W. Stott (New York: Fortress Press, 2008), 89.
2. Eberhard Bethge, *Dietrich Bonhoeffer: A Biography*, rev. ed. (Minneapolis: Augsburg Fortress, 2000), 134.
3. *Barcelona, Berlin, New York: 1928–1931*, 139.

CHAPTER 4: TO AMERICA AND BACK

1. *Barcelona, Berlin, New York: 1928–1931*, vol. 10, *Dietrich Bonhoeffer Works*, ed. Clifford J. Green, trans. Douglas W. Stott (New York: Fortress Press, 2008), 265–66.
2. Ibid., 308.
3. Ibid., 309–10.
4. Ibid., 293.
5. Wolf-Dieter Zimmermann and Ronald G. Smith, eds., *I Knew Dietrich Bonhoeffer*, trans. Käthe Gregor Smith (New York: Harper and Row, 1966), 60.
6. Inge Karding, interview by Martin Doblmeier, *Bonhoeffer: Pastor, Pacifist, Nazi Resister. A documentary film by Martin Doblmeier*, Princeton University. Unused footage quoted here by permission of the director.
7. Zimmermann and Smith, *I Knew Dietrich Bonhoeffer*, 64–65.

CHAPTER 5: NAZI THEOLOGY AND THE FÜHRER PRINCIPLE

1. *No Rusty Swords: Letters, Lectures and Notes 1928–1936*, vol. 1, *Collected Works of Dietrich Bonhoeffer*, ed. Edwin H. Robertson, trans. Edwin H. Robertson and John Bowden (New York: Harper and Row, 1965), 203–04.
2. Eberhard Bethge, *Dietrich Bonhoeffer: A Biography*, rev. ed. (Minneapolis: Augsburg Fortress, 2000), 258.
3. Ibid., 257.
4. Mary Bosanquet, *The Life and Death of Dietrich Bonhoeffer* (New York: Harper and Row, 1968), 117.
5. William L. Shirer, *The Rise and Fall of the Third Reich: A History of Nazi Germany* (New York: Simon and Schuster, 1960), 194.
6. Sabine Leibholz-Bonhoeffer, *The Bonhoeffers: Portrait of a Family* (New York: St. Martin's Press, 1971), 84.

CHAPTER 6: THE CHURCH STRUGGLE

1. Adolf Hitler, "Concordat Between the Holy See and the German Reich [With Supplementary Protocol and Secret Supplement]," July 20, 1933, trans., Muriel Frasier, http://www.concordatwatch.eu/showkb .php?org_id=858&kb_header_id=752&kb_id=1211.
2. Eberhard Bethge, *Dietrich Bonhoeffer: A Biography*, rev. ed. (Minneapolis: Augsburg Fortress, 2000), 301.
3. *London: 1933-1935*, vol. 13, *Dietrich Bonhoeffer Works*, ed. Keith Clements, trans. Isabel Best (New York: Fortress Press, 2007), 23.
4. Ibid., 39–41.
5. Ibid., 97–98.
6. Ibid., 129.
7. Ibid., 179–80.
8. William L. Shirer, *The Rise and Fall of the Third Reich: A History of Nazi Germany* (New York: Simon and Schuster, 1960), 226.

CHAPTER 7: ZINGST AND FINKENWALDE

1. Wolf-Dieter Zimmermann and Ronald G. Smith, eds., *I Knew Dietrich Bonhoeffer*, trans. Käthe Gregor Smith (New York: Harper and Row, 1966), 91.

2. Eberhard Bethge, *Dietrich Bonhoeffer: A Biography*, rev. ed. (Minneapolis: Augsburg Fortress, 2000), 479.
3. *London: 1933-1935*, vol. 13, *Dietrich Bonhoeffer Works*, ed. Keith Clements, trans. Isabel Best (New York: Fortress Press, 2007), 308–09.
4. Ibid., 217–18.
5. Ibid., 396.
6. Albrecht Schönherr, interview by Martin Doblmeier, *Bonhoeffer: Pastor, Pacifist, Nazi Resister. A documentary film by Martin Doblmeier*, Princeton University. Unused footage quoted here by permission of the director.
7. Germany, *Nuremberg Laws*, September 15, 1935.
8. Bethge, *Dietrich Bonhoeffer: A Biography*, 512.
9. *The Way to Freedom: Letters, Lectures and Notes 1935–1939*, vol. 2, *Collected Works of Dietrich Bonhoeffer*, ed. Edwin H. Robertson, trans. Edwin H. Robertson and John Bowden (New York: Harper and Row, 1966), 110.
10. Ibid., 149.
11. Ibid., 151.
12. Bethge, *Dietrich Bonhoeffer: A Biography*, 591.

CHAPTER 8: THE GREAT DECISION

1. Eberhard Bethge, *Dietrich Bonhoeffer: A Biography*, rev. ed. (Minneapolis: Augsburg Fortress, 2000), 602.
2. Sabine Leibholz-Bonhoeffer, *The Bonhoeffers: Portrait of a Family* (New York: St. Martin's Press, 1971), 97–100.
3. *The Way to Freedom: Letters, Lectures and Notes 1935–1939*, vol. 2, *Collected Works of Dietrich Bonhoeffer*, ed. Edwin H. Robertson, trans. Edwin H. Robertson and John Bowden (New York: Harper and Row, 1966), 228–229.
4. Ibid., 230.
5. Ibid., 233–34.
6. Mary Bosanquet, *The Life and Death of Dietrich Bonhoeffer* (New York: Harper and Row, 1968), 217–18.
7. Wolf-Dieter Zimmermann and Ronald G. Smith, eds., *I Knew Dietrich Bonhoeffer*, trans. Käthe Gregor Smith (New York: Harper and Row, 1966), 158–60.
8. Albrecht Schönherr, interview by Martin Doblmeier, *Bonhoeffer: Pastor, Pacifist, Nazi Resister. A documentary film* by Martin Doblmeier, date of interview, Princeton University. Unused footage quoted here by permission of the director.

CHAPTER 9: FROM CONFESSION TO CONSPIRACY

1. Eberhard Bethge, *Friendship and Resistance: Essays on Dietrich Bonhoeffer* (Grand Rapids: Eerdmans, 1995), 24.
2. *Conspiracy and Imprisonment: 1940–1945*, vol. 16, *Dietrich Bonhoeffer Works*, ed. Mark S. Brocker, trans. Lisa E. Dahill with Douglas W. Stott (New York: Fortress Press, 2006), 106.
3. Ibid., 207–08.

CHAPTER 10: BONHOEFFER IN LOVE

1. Ruth-Alice von Bismarck and Ulrich Kabitz, eds., *Love Letters from Cell 92: The Correspondence Between Dietrich Bonhoeffer and Maria Von Wedemeyer, 1943–45*, trans. John Brownjohn (New York: Abingdon Press, 1995), 330.
2. *Conspiracy and Imprisonment: 1940–1945*, vol. 16, *Dietrich Bonhoeffer Works*, ed. Mark S. Brocker, trans. Lisa E. Dahill with Douglas W. Stott (New York: Fortress Press, 2006), 329–30.
3. Bismarck and Kabitz, *Love Letters from Cell 92*, 331–32.
4. *Conspiracy and Imprisonment*, 366–67.
5. Ibid., 369–70.
6. Ibid., 370–71.
7. Ibid., 373–74.
8. Bismarck and Kabitz, *Love Letters from Cell 92*, 336.
9. Ibid., 337.
10. Ibid.
11. Ibid., 338–39.
12. *Conspiracy and Imprisonment*, 383–84.
13. Ibid., 390.

CHAPTER 11: CELL 92 AT TEGEL PRISON

1. Wolf-Dieter Zimmermann and Ronald G. Smith, eds., *I Knew Dietrich Bonhoeffer*, trans. Käthe Gregor Smith (New York: Harper and Row, 1966), 190–92.
2. Mary Bosanquet, *The Life and Death of Dietrich Bonhoeffer* (New York: Harper and Row, 1968), 247–48.
3. *Letters and Papers from Prison*, vol. 8, *Dietrich Bonhoeffer Works*, ed. John W. Degruchy (Minneapolis: Augsburg Fortress, 2010), 21–22.
4. Ibid., 189.
5. Ibid., 163.
6. Ruth-Alice von Bismarck and Ulrich Kabitz, eds., *Love Letters from Cell 92: The Correspondence Between Dietrich Bonhoeffer and Maria Von Wedemeyer, 1943–45*, trans. John Brownjohn (New York: Abingdon Press, 1995), 26–27.
7. Ibid., 33–34.
8. *Letters and Papers from Prison*, 144–45.
9. William L. Shirer, *The Rise and Fall of the Third Reich: A History of Nazi Germany* (New York: Simon and Schuster, 1960), 1069.
10. Joachim Fest, *Plotting Hitler's Death: The German Resistance to Hitler, 1933–1945*, trans. Bruce Little (New York: Metropolitan Books, 1996), 289–90.
11. Bismarck and Kabitz, *Love Letters from Cell 92*, 261–62.
12. Ibid., 268–70.

CHAPTER 12: ON THE ROAD TO FREEDOM

1. Wolf-Dieter Zimmermann and Ronald G. Smith, eds., *I Knew Dietrich Bonhoeffer*, trans. Käthe Gregor Smith (New York: Harper and Row, 1966), 226–30.
2. S. Payne Best, *The Venlo Incident* (Watford, Herts: Hutchinson, 1950), 179.
3. Ibid., 192.

4. Ibid., 195–96.
5. Sabine Leibholz-Bonhoeffer, *The Bonhoeffers: Portrait of a Family*, (New York: St. Martin's Press, 1971), 198–99.
6. Best, *The Venlo Incident*, 200.
7. Eberhard Bethge, *Dietrich Bonhoeffer: A Biography*, rev. ed. (Minneapolis: Augsburg Fortress, 2000), 927–28.

EPILOGUE
1. Sabine Leibholz-Bonhoeffer, *The Bonhoeffers: Portrait of a Family* (New York: St. Martin's Press, 1971), 184–86.
2. Ibid., 190.
3. Ibid., 187–88.
4. Ibid., 188.
5. Ibid., 188–89.
6. Amos Cresswell and Maxwell Tow, *Dr. Franz Hildebrandt: Mr. Valiant for Truth* (Grand Rapids: Smyth and Helwys, 2000), 223–27.

BIBLIOGRAPHY

Bailey, J. M., and Douglas Gilbert. *The Steps of Bonhoeffer: A Pictorial Album*. Philadelphia: Pilgrim Press, 1969.

Barnett, Victoria. *For the Soul of the People: Protestant Protest against Hitler*. New York: Oxford University Press, 1992.

Bassett, Richard. *Hitler's Spy Chief: The Wilhelm Canaris Mystery*. London: Cassell, 2005.

Bentley, James. *Martin Niemöller 1892–1984*. New York: Free Press, 1984.

Bergen, Doris L. *Twisted Cross: The German Christian Movement in the Third Reich*. Chapel Hill: University of North Carolina Press, 1996.

Best, S. Payne. *The Venlo Incident*. Watford, Herts: Hutchinson & Co., 1950.

Bethge, Eberhard. *Dietrich Bonhoeffer: A Biography*. Minneapolis: Fortress Press, 1967.

———. *Dietrich Bonhoeffer: Man of Vision, Man of Courage*. Edited by Edwin Robertson. New York: Harper and Row, 1970.

———. *Friendship and Resistance: Essays on Dietrich Bonhoeffer*. Chicago: World Council of Churches, 1995.

———. *Friendship and Resistance: Essays on Dietrich Bonhoeffer*. Grand Rapids: Eerdmans, 1995.

Bethge, Renate, and Christian Gremmels, eds. *Dietrich Bonhoeffer: A Life in Pictures*. Centenary ed. Translated by Brian McNeil. Minneapolis: Fortress Press, 2006.

Bethge, Renate. *Dietrich Bonhoeffer: A Brief Life*. New York: Fortress Press, 2004.

Bird, Eugene K. *Prisoner #7: Rudolf Hess: The Thirty Years in Jail of Hitler's Deputy Führer*. New York: Viking Press, 1974.

Bonhoeffer, Dietrich. *A Testament to Freedom: The Essential Writings of Dietrich Bonhoeffer*. rev. ed. Edited by Geffrey B. Kelly and F. Burton Nelson. New York: Harper One, 1995.

———. *Christ the Center*. Translated by Edwin H. Robertson. New York: Harper San Francisco, 1978.

———. *Collected Works of Dietrich Bonhoeffer*. Edited by Edwin H. Robertson. 3 vols. New York: Harper and Row, 1965–1973.

———. *Creation and Fall: A Theological Exposition of Genesis 1–3*. Edited by John W. De Gruchy. Translated by Douglas S. Bax. New York: Fortress Press, 1997.

———. *Dietrich Bonhoeffer Works Series*. Edited by Victoria J. Barnett and Barbara Wojhoski. 16 vols. Minneapolis: Augsburg Fortress, 1995–2010.

Bosanquet, Mary. *The Life and Death of Dietrich Bonhoeffer*. New York: Harper and Row, 1968.

Cresswell, Amos, and Maxwell Tow. *Dr. Franz Hildebrandt: Mr. Valiant for Truth*. Grand Rapids: Smyth and Helwys, 2000.

De Gruchy, John W. *Daring, Trusting Spirit: Bonhoeffer's Friend Eberhard Bethge*. Minneapolis: Augsburg Fortress, 2005.

De Gruchy, John W., ed. *The Cambridge Companion to Dietrich Bonhoeffer*. New York: Cambridge University Press, 1999.

Fest, Joachim C. *Plotting Hitler's Death: The German Resistance to Hitler, 1933–1945*. Translated by Bruce Little. New York: Metropolitan Books, 1996.

Gaevernitz, Gero V. S., ed. *They Almost Killed Hitler*. New York: Macmillan, 1947.

Galante, Pierre, and Eugene Silianoff. *Operation Valkyrie: The German Generals' Plot against Hitler*. Translated by Mark Howson and Cary Ryan. New York: Harper and Row, 1981.

Gill, Theodore A. *Memo for a Movie: A Short Life of Dietrich Bonhoeffer*. New York: Macmillan, 1971.

Gisevius, Hans B. *To the Bitter End: An Insider's Account of the Plot to Kill Hitler, 1933–1944*. Translated by Richard Winston and Clara Winston. New York: Da Capo Press, 1998.

Goddard, Donald. *The Last Days of Dietrich Bonhoeffer*. New York: Harper and Row, 1976.

Haynes, Stephen R. *The Bonhoeffer Phenomenon: Post-Holocaust Perspectives*. New York: Fortress Press, 2004.

Huntemann, Georg. *The Other Bonhoeffer: An Evangelical Reassessment of Dietrich Bonhoeffer*. Translated by Todd Huizinga. Grand Rapids: Baker, 1993.

Kelly, Geffrey B., F. Burton Nelson, and Renate Bethge. *The Cost of Moral Leadership: The Spirituality of Dietrich Bonhoeffer*. Boston: Eerdmans, 2002.

Kleinhans, Theodore J. *Till the Night Be Past: The Life and Times of Dietrich Bonhoeffer*. New York: Concordia House, 2002.

Kuhns, William. *In Pursuit of Dietrich Bonhoeffer*. Dayton: Pflaum Press, 1967.

Lean, Garth. *On the Tail of a Comet: The Life of Frank Buchman*. New York: Helmers and Howard, 1988.

Leibholz-Bonhoeffer, Sabine. *The Bonhoeffers: Portrait of a Family*. New York: St. Martin's Press, 1971.

Lochner, Louis P., ed. *The Goebbels Diaries 1942–1943*. Garden City, NY: Doubleday, 1948.

Machtan, Lothar. *Hidden Hitler*. Translated by John Brownjohn and Susanne Ehlert. New York: Basic Books, 2001.

Marty, Martin E., ed. *The Place of Bonhoeffer: Problems and Possibilities in His Thought*. New York: Association Press, 1962.

Patten, Thomas E. *The Twisted Cross and Dietrich Bonhoeffer*. Lima, OH: Fairway Press, 1992.

Rasmussen, Larry L. *Dietrich Bonhoeffer: Reality and Resistance*. Studies in Christian Ethics Series. Nashville: Abingdon Press, 1972.

Raum, Elizabeth. *Dietrich Bonhoeffer: Called by God*. London: Burns and Oates, 2002.

Ritter, Gerhard. *The German Resistance: Carl Goerdeler's Struggle against Tyranny*. Translated by R. T. Clark. New York: Frederick A. Praeger, 1958.

Robertson, Edwin H. *The Shame and the Sacrifice: The Life and Martyrdom of Dietrich Bonhoeffer*. New York: Macmillan, 1988.

Shirer, William L. *The Rise and Fall of the Third Reich: A History of Nazi Germany*. New York: Simon and Schuster, 1960.

Sklar, Dusty. *The Nazis and the Occult*. New York: Dorset Press, 1977.

Slane, Craig J. *Bonhoeffer as Martyr: Social Responsibility and Modern Christian Commitment*. New York: Brazos Press, 2004.

Speer, Albert. *Inside the Third Reich: Memoirs by Albert Speer*. Translated by Richard Winston and Clara Winston. New York: Macmillan, 1970.

Steigmann-Gall, Richard. *The Holy Reich: Nazi Conceptions of Christianity, 1919–1945*. Cambridge: Cambridge University Press, 2003.

Von Bismarck, Ruth-Alice, and Ulrich Kabitz, eds. *Love Letters from Cell 92: The Correspondence Between Dietrich Bonhoeffer and Maria Von Wedemeyer, 1943–45*. Translated by John Brownjohn. New York: Abingdon Press, 1995.

Wind, Renate. *Dietrich Bonhoeffer: A Spoke in the Wheel*. Translated by John Bowden. Grand Rapids: Eerdmans, 2002.

Wustenberg, Ralf K. *A Theology of Life: Dietrich Bonhoeffer's Religionless Christianity*. Translated by Douglas Stott. Grand Rapids: Eerdmans, 1998.

Zimmermann, Wolf-Dieter, and Ronald G. Smith, eds. *I Knew Dietrich Bonhoeffer*. Translated by Käthe G. Smith. New York: Harper and Row, 1966.

INDEX

Buchenwald, 197–201, 202, 204–05, 212

C

Canaris, Wilhelm, 124–25, 134–35, 141, 144–45, 176, 183, 187, 191, 209

Catholicism, 24–25, 75–76, 101, 105, 126, 140, 142–43

Central Bureau of Interchurch Aid, 126

Chamberlain, Neville (Brit. prime minister), 122–23, 126, 133–34

Charlottenburg (Berlin), xii, 171

"cheap grace," 6, 111–12, 122–23

Chronicle of Shame (file), 125, 188–89

church and the Jewish question, 62–63

"Church and the Jewish Question, The" (Bonhoeffer), 62–63

church elections, 75–76

Churchill, Winston, x–xi, 147

church struggle, 73–91, 99–105

collective pastorates, 115–116, 133, 135

Columbus (German ship), 41

Commissar Order, 144–45

concentration camps, xi, 61, 133, 187, 188, 197, 201, 212. *See also* Buchenwald; Flossenbürg; Sachsenhausen

Confessing Church, 79, 86, 88–91, 98, 100–01, 106–07, 109–120, 132, 137–38, 141, 143–45, 148

Confessional Movement (Confessing Movement), 90, 110

Confessional Synod of the German Evangelical Church, 99

Cost of Discipleship, The (Bohnoeffer), 115, 178

Czech resistance to Nazi occupation, 150

Czeppan, Maria, 169

D

Dahlem Resolution, 99

Das Gebetbook der Bibel (The Prayerbook of the Bible) (Bonhoeffer), 140

Deissman, Adolf, 27

Delbrück, Emmi. *See* Bonhoeffer, Emmi (Delbrück)

Diestel, Max, 41, 44

disabled: Bethel community for, 77; Hitler's view toward, 77; murder of, 136

Dilthey, Wilhelm, 177

discipleship, 214

Discipleship (Bonhoeffer). *See* Cost of Discipleship, The

dogmatics, 44

Dohnanyi, Christoph von, 175

Dohnanyi, Hans von, 60, 62, 92, 99, 106, 114, 120–21, 124–25, 135–36, 137–38, 141–42, 144–45, 148, 150, 153, 168–71, 175–76, 188, 192, 196, 198, 208

Dolchtoss (stab-in-the-back), 14, 136

Dudzus, Otto, 97–98

E

ecumenical movement, 27, 48, 111–12, 125

Einsatzgruppen (SS paramilitary), 125, 145

Einstein, Albert, 66

Eliot, T. S., 83

Enabling Act, 61, 63

Epistle to the Romans, The (Barth), 27

Ettal Abbey (Benedictine Monastery), 142–43, 168, 178

Euthanasia Program. *See* T-4 euthanasia program

Evangelical Youth, 85

Evangelische Theologie, 110

Hildebrandt, Franz, 38, 62, 74,
  78–79, 83, 100, 106, 113–14,
  123, 126, 131, 212, 214
Himmler, Heinrich, 68, 123, 142,
  192, 199
Hindenburg, Paul von, 14, 61, 86,
  87, 92–93, 170
historical-critical method (aka
  "higher criticism"), 27–28
Hitler, Adolf: announcement of
  intent to attack Belgium,
  Holland, France, England,
  Norway, Denmark, 136;
  assassination attempts on,
  169, 183–89; attack on
  Holland, 139; attack on
  Russia, 145; attitude toward
  Christianity, 55; attitude
  toward the disabled, 77;
  Bierhall Putsch of, 22, 57, 92;
  conspiracy against, 136–50,
  164, 167–69, 175–76, 183–
  89; election of (as Reich
  chancellor), 55; oath of
  obedience to (for German
  pastors), 80; on Jesus, 67;
  plans for the church, 67–69;
  plans to attach Austria and
  Czechoslovakia, 118, 120;
  proposal of the office of
  Reichsbischof, 69–70; suicide of,
  211; takeover of the German
  military, 118–19
Höhle, Herr (Gestapo official),
  113
Holl, Karl, 27, 214
Holland: Hitler's attack on, 139
Holy Trinity Brompton Church
  (London), xi, 212–13
Horn, Käthe van, 3–5
Horn, Maria van, 3–4
"Horst Wessel Song" (Nazis' official
  anthem), 139

I

I Knew Dietrich Bonhoeffer
  (Schlabrendorff), 195–97
intercourse between Jews and
  Germans, 106
Iron Cross, 73
Islam, 55

J

Jacobi, Gerhard, 50, 83, 88, 100,
  111,
Jäger, August, 89
Japan: attack on Pearl Harbor, 149
Jensen, Hans-Werner, 107–08, 122,
  124
Jews: abductions of, 120;
  banned from cultural and
  entertainment activities,
  65; beginning of Hitler's
  persecution of, 62–63; deadly
  beatings of (Lithuania), 147;
  expelled from the world of
  journalism, 65; forbidden to
  display the Reich national
  flag or colors, 106; forbidden
  to employ female Germans
  ages 45 or less, 106; forbidden
  to marry Germans, 105–06;
  Hitler's boycott of businesses
  owned by, 63–64; in the
  concentration camps, 133;
  law prohibiting extramarital
  intercourse with Germans, 106;
  Luther and, 38–40; numbers
  limited in public schools, 65;
  Nuremburg Laws, 105–06;
  prohibited from serving as
  patent lawyers or as doctors
  in institutions with state-run
  insurance, 65; prohibitions
  expanded to include spouses
  of, 65; requirement to wear the
  yellow star, 148

ABOUT THE AUTHOR

E ric Metaxas is the author of the *New York Times* #1 bestseller
*Bonhoeffer: Pastor, Martyr, Prophet, Spy; Amazing Grace: William
Wilberforce and the Heroic Campaign to End Slavery; Seven Men and
the Secret of their Greatness;* and *Miracles: What They Are, Why
They Happen, and How They Can Change your Life.* ABC News has called
Metaxas a "photogenic, witty ambassador for faith in public life."
He was the keynote speaker at the 2012 National Prayer Breakfast
in Washington, D.C., and is a Senior Fellow at the King's College in
New York City, where he lives with his wife and daughter.